Y0-BQV-139

Christian Nurture Through The Church

BY LEE J. GABLE

Administering the Educational Work of the Church

National Council of the Churches of Christ in the U.S.A.

Published for
The Department of Administration and Leadership
Division of Christian Education
National Council of the Churches of Christ in the U.S.A.
by The P and D Department
120 East 23rd Street, New York 10, N. Y.

BB06-771 Price: $1.25 Printed in the U.S.A.

CONTENTS

FOREWORD

HERE is a book designed to make possible better Christian nurture—a book designed to help church school superintendents, directors of Christian education, pastors, field workers, and college and seminary classes.

The author, professor of Christian education at the Theological Seminary of the Evangelical and Reformed Church in Lancaster, Pennsylvania, writes out of experience as a leader in Christian education, not only in the local church but as a state and national leader. Among the capacities in which he has served are those of secretary in a state council of education, director of leadership education on a national denominational staff, director of leadership education and church school administration in the International Council of Religious Education and, later, in the National Council of Churches.

However, the book is the outgrowth not only of the author's rich experience but of the corporate thinking of seventy specialists in Christian education who gathered at Williams Bay, Wisconsin, in August, 1953, with the eventual production of this book as one of the desired outcomes.

Christian Nurture Through the Church draws upon the resources of many minds and reaches out to greet other minds—yours, for example; the minds of persons to whom you lend this book; the minds of those who work and learn in your church school.

These chapters can help tremendously in providing better facilities for Christian education. But, at best, they can only help. What is most needed is a person who will take seriously the urgent, searching question: "How can my church become a worthy channel of the Holy Spirit in Christian nurture?"

—GERALD E. KNOFF, *executive secretary*
DIVISION OF CHRISTIAN EDUCATION

National Council of the Churches of
Christ in the U.S.A.

CHAPTER I

Christian Nurture and the Task of the Church

What Is Christian Nurture?

By Christian nurture we mean *the total effort of the church to help each person to dedicate himself to Christ and to develop the understandings, the attitudes and the skills that he needs in order to be Christian in his personal life and in his relations with others.*

We use the term, "Christian nurture," rather than the more familiar term, "Christian education," for a reason that has nothing to do with the essential meaning of either term. As a matter of fact, the two terms may be used interchangeably, and we shall often refer to "educational" process and organization. We are concerned in these pages with the task of the church to help its people grow as Christians. This is the task of the whole church, not of certain parts of the church. For some people Christian education has come to mean only a part of the church, such as, the "Sunday school." They feel that the rest of the church program is not meant to be educational and that other church groups have no responsibility for Christian education. The term, "Christian nurture," has not been so limited in the thinking of people. Therefore, we shall use it in the hope that every person who reads these pages will see his own share in a program of Christian nurture which is the task of the church as a whole.

As it seeks to fulfill this task the church must constantly keep two concerns at the heart of all its work. One concern is its *heritage as a Church of Jesus Christ.* It has inherited God's revelation of himself as Creator of all things and Father of all mankind. It has inherited faith in Jesus Christ as Savior and Lord. It has inherited its mission as a fellowship of committed people. In all that it does it must be true to this revelation, this faith, and this mission.

The other concern is for the person—*each person.* No two people are altogether alike. Each has his own age, his interests, his abilities, his background, his feelings, his motives. The church fulfills its task only as it helps each person to become dedicated to Christ and to develop Christian understandings, attitudes, and skills.

The church which thinks only of heritage is in danger of going through motions and ceremonies whose real meaning has been lost somewhere in the past. The church which thinks only of people is in danger of becoming merely a "club" whose members like each other but which has little Christian impact on persons or on society. The true Church of Jesus Christ helps its heritage to come alive and remain alive in the experience of its people.

Urgency of the Task

The task of the church is not one to be taken lightly. It is urgent. Each person is important. Each person, whatever his age, is at a period that is crucial for his life. The child is forming attitudes that will be with him as long as he lives and that he can change only with increasing difficulty. It is important for him and his future that he grow in the atmosphere of a Christian home and that he and his family feel constantly the influence of the church. The critical adjustments and decisions of youth confront the church and the home with a responsibility that is just as urgent and just as personal as that of childhood.

The responsibility changes with the coming of adult years, but the urgency remains. Men and women need the constant nurture of the church if they are to fulfill as Christians the changing tasks of vocation, family, citizenship, and personal adjustment. In each of these ages and in each of these tasks, every person needs the church in order that he may give the witness of a committed follower of Jesus Christ.

The task of the church is urgent because of the kind of world in which we live. It is a steadily shrinking world. Each time the inventive skill of man speeds up travel or communication, the world becomes smaller for practical purposes. Every person in the world becomes a nearer neighbor. It is urgent that this shrinking world become a Christian neighborhood.

This is an interdependent world. The political trends in one country affect the peace and security of every other. The manufacturers of one country affect the economy of many others. The day has passed when any country can rest secure behind its oceans or mountains, without caring what happens on the other side. For good or ill, the world is linked in partnership. It is important that all of these world-partners be people and nations on whom the others can safely rely.

With this shrinkage and growing dependence has come a fearful development of power. As these pages are being written it has become necessary to use new words to express the force which man is now able to develop. Thus far this force has been developed largely for purposes of destruction. Each nation watches the others, fearful of the power they may develop, and fearful that a careless act somewhere may bring catastrophe to all.

Let no pharisaism creep into the church. The unchristian attitudes and actions that concern us are found on both sides of every ocean. They are in city, suburb, town, and country. They may be found in overprivileged and in underprivileged communities. Delinquency may be outside the church or inside. Wherever there is selfishness, false pride, prejudice, dishonesty—there the Church of Jesus Christ has an urgent task.

The only good answer for a world like this is fuller acceptance of Jesus Christ as Lord and Savior. If a man lives by the spirit of Jesus Christ he can be trusted as a neighbor. If the spirit of Jesus Christ controls the responsible leaders of business, industry, government, and all the other operations of society, then and only then can the world find security. There is, therefore, new urgency in the Great Commission of Jesus: "Go therefore and make disciples of all nations, baptizing them in the name of the Father and of the Son and of the Holy Spirit, teaching them to observe all that I have commanded you" (Matthew 28:19-20). Part of this commission rests on every church school teacher, on every superintendent, pastor, director of Christian education, or member of a local church board of Christian education. This is our commission, and it needs our attention now.

The Task of the Whole Church

Christian nurture as we have defined it belongs to the whole church. Every church activity and every church organization should contribute to the Christian nurture of the people who are affected by it. If Christian nurture is not the result, there is real question as to whether that activity or that organization really belongs to the church.

A program of evangelism, for example, is judged not only by the members who are added to the church rolls but by the numbers who are drawn into continuing and growing participation in the church. Worship is judged not merely by the way worship services are planned and conducted but by the true worship experience of leaders and participants alike. The every-member canvass is judged not only by the extent to which the church budget is subscribed but by the increased dedication of time and energy. The fellowship which members of the brotherhood enjoy is good only if they also gain a new sense of churchmanship. This means, then, that the church as a whole and also its various organizations have clear responsibility for Christian nurture.

Objectives of Christian Nurture

The church that seeks to bring the Christian heritage into the lives of people must think carefully of its objectives. People are different and they are at different stages of advancement, but the ultimate goal is the same for all of them. The church seeks to bring each of them into a conscious relationship to God as Father and to Jesus Christ as Savior and Lord. It seeks to draw them into responsible participation in the Christian family and in the Christian Church. It seeks to help them develop Christian faith and character which will result in Christian decisions and conduct.

The denominations, working together through the International Council of Religious Education, long ago agreed on a general statement of the objectives of Christian education. These objectives have helped curriculum writers to prepare adequate lesson materials. They have helped program planners to develop program guides. They have helped local church workers to recognize the responsibility which they have for the Christian nurture of persons.[1]

Any such statement is, of course, intended for guidance only and is not to be imposed on a church or church group. Each group should give thought to its own objectives. Let each group be sure, however, that the essentials of the Christian faith and life are covered. Objectives of Christian nurture for any church should include such essential elements as: belief in God and relationship to him, acceptance of Jesus Christ, the Bible, the Church, personal Christian living, the person and his role in society, and a Christian philosophy of life.

Workers with children soon found that they had to interpret these general objectives according to the stages of development through childhood. Teachers and curriculum writers needed to know how far along toward a particular goal a child of a given age ought to be. They needed to know how much progress to expect in a particular church school department. Therefore, they worked out a set of goals for the religious education of children. Junior high leaders did the same for their age group. Others followed.

We do not reproduce these age-group goals here, for they are subject to revision in the light of experience. The current forms of these goals are noted in the Appendix among the references used by the author. Age-group workers, curriculum writers, and program planners should be familiar with the most recent formulation of goals for the age-groups with which they are working.

---

[1] For the most recent statement of these objectives, write to the Division of Christian Education, National Council of Churches.

No statement of goals, however carefully prepared, will apply equally well to every church, every group, and every person. Just as a suit of clothes must be fitted to the person, so must the statement of goals for Christian nurture. It is necessary, therefore, for each individual leader to develop his own set of objectives.

Each teacher should be familiar with goals for Christian nurture in general and for his age group in particular. More specifically, each teacher should set his own objectives for each unit of work, and even for each session, adapting to his class or group the goals suggested in curriculum materials. The commission of Jesus Christ is for each of us as well as for the disciples who walked with him in the flesh. Part of that commission may be fulfilled in the next session of any group, if that group sees its goals clearly and works toward them effectively.

Some Factors That Affect Christian Nurture

Christian nurture does not take place in a vacuum. Nor does it take place under circumstances that obligingly remain the same. There are many factors that have a bearing on Christian nurture, and these factors are changing all the time. It is the task of the church administrator to weigh them.

Person-centered factors

The people of any church are of different ages, with varying interests, abilities, and needs. They come from varying home and family backgrounds. There are different cultural levels, moral standards, and degrees of religious spirit and insight. No amount of wishful thinking on the part of the administrator will make these people alike. They are what they are. The church takes them as it finds them, and then seeks to develop a program broad enough and varied enough to bring about Christian growth in each of them.

These people move about a great deal more than they used to do. It has been reported, for example, that in 1950 more than 19 million people moved to a new location within the same county and that more than eight and a quarter million moved outside the county. Christian nurture is just as important for the person who moves as for the person who remains in one location. It is difficult, however, for the church to provide Christian nurture for those who move.

Large numbers of people move, even though they keep the same address. "Week-end mobility" is here as a result of the increasing number of automobiles and of the shorter work week. On one long holiday week end, it was reported that 40 million automobiles were on American highways. That Sunday was a hard one for educational leaders in American churches!

Suburban life, with husbands working at factories and offices some miles from home, represents another kind of travel. The suburban husband cannot attend an early evening meeting. In fact, he may be hard to reach for any evening meeting, regardless of the time it begins.

Church-centered factors

Part of the heritage which a church brings to its people is membership in a denomination. The history of that denomination enriches every one of its congregations and every one of its members. If there is a neighboring church of the same denomination, the two may strengthen each other through fellowship and joint enterprises. Then there is the extensive list of services which each denomination offers—church school curriculum, program helps, field staff service, co-operation with other denominations in developing plans and materials which benefit everyone.

Each congregation has within itself certain factors that affect the Christian growth of those whom it touches. These factors are so numerous that they cannot be listed with profit. They are not necessarily good or bad, but they make a difference. In size, the congregation may be very small or very large. In form of worship it may be liturgical or free. Economically it may be rich or poor. Spiritually it may be vital or sluggish. It may be located in city, suburb, town, or open country. It may have high standing as "the church" in the community, or it may be the small church overshadowed by its more impressive neighbor. It may rely on a reputation inherited from a past generation, or it may be creating its own reputation now.

The program of each church is affected by its neighboring churches. There may be co-operation through an organized council of churches or through informal fellowship. In either case co-operating churches help each other. In fact, the stronger a co-operating church becomes the more it helps its neighbors. There may be competition among churches even though a council exists on paper. Competition may make a church alert. It may even help a church statistically. It is doubtful, however, if an effort to beat a neighboring church has much value spiritually. The formation of the World Council of Churches and of the National Council of Churches has greatly strengthened the positive influence of church co-operation.

Community-centered factors

There are deep-seated differences among communities, and these differences reveal factors that influence Christian nurture. Is it an old community, with patterns of church life that are established and hard to change? Is it a new community in which the church is just now being established, and in which little is fixed and dependable? Is it predominantly Protestant, predominantly Roman Catholic, predominantly Jewish, or mixed? Has there been an influx of different racial groups? Is it declining in size and importance, growing in size and importance, or static? Different patterns of work will be needed, depending on the nature of the community. The mood of the people and the strength and flexibility of the church will vary from one of these types to another.

National and international factors

National and international situations make a difference. The mood of people, the needs of people, the numbers of people available for church activity are different in times of war and in times of peace. Economic stability makes a difference, as those who remember periods of depression can testify. American traditions of separation of church and state make the program of the church free from direct government intervention. The stability and integrity of the national administration, however, can and do make a difference in the work of the church. The church and its objectives do not change with the passing of political regimes. There is abundant evidence, however, to show that national and international factors make a difference in the way a church undertakes its task.

CHAPTER II

How Christian Nurture Takes Place

He who would go on a journey needs a map. He who would build a building needs a blueprint. He who would make a suit needs a pattern. He who would bake a cake needs a recipe. He who would lead a church in Christian nurture needs to analyze his task in the same fashion as did those who prepared the blueprint, the pattern, and the recipe. What are the essentials to Christian nurture? What ideas are so important in Christian nurture that *with* them we succeed, and *without* them we fail?

Jesus Christ is the one by whom the Christian experience of persons and groups is measured

In a society as complex as ours it is hard to be sure what is right. No one can understand all the pressures and all the influences that bear upon him. No one, by his own wisdom, can foresee the possible effects of each of them, and choose wisely.

For the Christian, Jesus Christ provides the standard. If we know what Jesus did under circumstances like our own, we have clear guidance. The trouble is that in many respects our world is different from the world of Jesus. He faced a different set of social, political, and economic conditions from those that confront us. This does not, however, change the fact that the Christian is committed to Jesus Christ as Savior and Lord. It simply makes our choices the more difficult. We need to remember that this is God's world and that Jesus is the most complete revelation of God to man. We must make an honest and a reverent attempt to determine what Jesus would do if he were living in our circumstances. We must try sincerely to follow that course. This is not easy, nor is it comfortable, but the way of Jesus has never been either easy or comfortable.

The Holy Spirit regenerates men and brings about the development of Christian character and conduct

The church does not produce Christian commitment nor does it develop Christian character in people. These are the work of the Holy

Spirit. All the church can do is to establish conditions favorable to the working of the Spirit. The church can help people to recognize their need and to be open to the Spirit. It is the function of worship and of evangelism to develop this readiness. It is also the function of Christian nurture to do so. The teacher and group leader must recognize the presence of the Holy Spirit as active in the persons they teach. Teaching, then, is a divine-human partnership.

The Bible is our unique spiritual resource and is a necessary aid to Christian growth

It is not necessary for each generation to "start from scratch" in discovering the Christian faith. We have a record of God's revelation of himself and of man's response to that revelation. Many a man in many a generation has said with the Psalmist, "Thy word is a lamp to my feet and a light to my path" (Psalm 119:105). As Christians we find our inspiration and empowerment for Christian living in the New Testament, and primarily in Jesus Christ.

The Church, therefore, in providing Christian nurture for its people, must lead them to use, understand, and appreciate the Bible as basic to their life and faith.

Christian nurture must take into account the dual nature of man

The efforts of the church in Christian nurture would be simplified if man were either clearly good or clearly bad. The trouble is that man is both! He has capacity for good, and at the same time, tendency toward evil.

According to the Genesis account of creation, "God created man in his own image, in the image of God he created him" (1:27). Clearly this cannot refer to any physical likeness. It can mean only a spiritual or qualitative likeness. If this be true at all, it can mean only that man can change from the state in which he is at any particular time and grow toward Godlikeness. Many of the recorded sayings of Jesus point in the same direction. For example, "You, therefore, must be perfect, as your heavenly Father is perfect" (Matthew 5:48). Jesus put great stress on the capacity of man for good.

The tendency toward evil is just as real. Far back in religious history the doctrine of the "fall" of man was used to account for the evil in him. If we leap across the centuries, with all of the progress that they have brought, we still see man committing crimes, fighting wars, building only to destroy. The writer of Romans had an insight that is true of every generation when he wrote, "I can will what is right, but I cannot do it. For I do not do the good I want, but the evil I do not want is what I do" (Romans 7:18b-19).

Christian nurture meets persons at the point of their underlying needs

Jesus approached persons and presented his call to discipleship in terms of immediate activities, but he always went beneath the surface experience to the underlying spiritual need. The current experience was a useful starting point, but he was concerned to get beneath it to the real need which could be discerned in terms of God's demands upon people. Thus he talked with the Samaritan woman about her need for that which was more enduring than the water she had come to get. Thus he did not merely talk to Zacchaeus about his desire for a glimpse of Jesus but of that which was far deeper. Thus he went beyond the question of the rich young ruler to the problem which was his real need.

Each of these persons had his own particular problems, his own particular expression of a fundamental need. He could be reached only in the particular experience, but the teaching of Jesus never stopped with this nor offered any superficial solution. He always went to the radical difficulty and offered the radical answer. So our efforts at Christian nurture must be based on a knowledge of man's profound need for reconciliation with God and must proceed in the light of current experience. Nurture must always start where the person is and be concerned with his expressed needs and interests. It can never stop, if it is Christian nurture, without bringing the person to a sense of his deepest need and making him aware of the possibility of the meeting of this need for God, through faith in Jesus Christ.

Jesus did not interpret a different God to each of these persons. He did not hold a different faith before each of them. The ultimate goal for each was the same. But the route by which each was to reach that goal was different. Each person had his own reason for being interested in Jesus and his way. Each had his own particular need, his own particular problems. Each brought his own particular contribution to the company of disciples. Therefore, Jesus centered his ministry to people on their current experience.

When we say that the program of Christian nurture centers on the current Christian experience of people, we are simply doing what Jesus did. We are by no means substituting something else for the Bible or for the Christian faith. Rather we are saying that he who leads in Christian nurture must find the way by which the Christian faith can be made vital to any particular person or group.

Nurture and growth go on all the time

There is no law by which Christian growth shall take place only between nine and twelve on Sunday mornings. In every waking moment something happens to the understandings, attitudes, and skills of people. We are changed in church, on the playground, at work, through television, on vacation trips, around the dinner table. Some of the changes are the result of planned teaching. Others spring from entirely unplanned experiences. Some of the changes mean progress toward Christian goals, and some away from Christian goals. The church must be concerned, therefore, with all the experiences a person has. It may seek to control these experiences, or to guide the person's reaction to them, but it cannot ignore them. Since many of these experiences are in the home, or may be controlled by the family, it is especially important that the church and the home work together in Christian nurture.

We learn what we live, to the extent that we accept it to live by

Here is a principle to which church leaders have given lip service but which they have followed too little in the full round of church work. Simply to hear a truth spoken is not necessarily to be changed by it. Nor is a person changed if he is able to repeat that truth well enough to pass an examination on it.

We have often used the word, "learning," to mean ability to put a particular truth or idea into words. By our definition, this is not Christian *nurture*. We have said that nurture should provide for understanding and attitudes and skills. A skill can be learned only through the practice of it. An attitude can be developed only when one is in a situation where that attitude can grow. Most of us would say that understanding, too, requires something deeper than the ability to put a truth or idea into words. Learning, then, is more than an intellectual exercise. It involves thinking and feeling and doing. We can be sure Christian learning has taken place when people have put Christian principles into practice.

We learn through experience in a group, as well as through the direct efforts of teacher or leader

How often have you heard a minister speak of "my church," or a teacher speak of "my class," or a chairman speak of "my committee"? The implication is that the leader rules the group, that the leader is important and that the group is unimportant. It is true, of course, that the skill and spirit of the leader have a profound influence on the group and its work. It is also true that the individuals are tremendously influenced by the groups of which they are parts. These influences may be constructive or destructive. Christian educators must be concerned, therefore, with the social climate or atmosphere of the groups in which the people of the church are involved.

It is an established fact that a conclusion reached through group discussion is better understood than one reached through acceptance of a statement made by the leader. The question or comment of one member of the group helps another to clarify his views. The question of a member who does not see the point clearly may bring out information the leader would not have thought to mention, though he knew it all the while.

The question or objection of a skeptical member of the group may help all the rest by giving them answers to questions they had not thought to raise.

A conclusion reached through a group process is not only better understood but more thoroughly carried out than one taken on the word of a leader. In many groups there is a degree of resistance to the leader. We do not like to "be told." People of any age are more ready to live by a conclusion they have formed themselves than by one which was suggested by someone else.

A group experience is rich in by-products. He who learns something as part of a group gains more than knowledge. He also enjoys fellowship, and his experience is the richer for it. He who learns something alone increases his knowledge. He who works with a group develops skill in group work and leadership in addition to knowledge. There are always extra values that come to the person who is part of a productive group.

Christian growth may take place through sudden change as well as by the slow, steady progress that we ordinarily associate with growth

There is no one road which everyone *must* travel to mature Christian faith and life. One, to quote the familiar phrase of Bushnell, may "grow up a Christian, and never know himself as being otherwise." Another may be able to trace his Christian commitment to some point where a sharp change took place in his life, or he may experience a sudden spurt in growth. For example, John Wesley, a clergyman in his mid-thirties, listened one evening to the reading of Luther's "Preface to the Epistle to the Romans." Later on, writing of this evening, he said, "About a quarter before nine, while he was describing the change which God works in the heart through faith in Christ, I felt my heart strangely warmed."

The church, in its educational efforts, has sought to develop steady growth-experiences. This is good. The church must not, however, overlook the possibility of sudden change, perhaps drastic change. The Christian heritage would be much the poorer without men like Zacchaeus, Paul, Augustine, and the host of others whose life took on new power and new direction quite unexpectedly.

Christian nurture calls for stirring the emotions as well as enlightening the mind

There is considerable wisdom in the story of the child who prayed, "God, help me to want to be as good as I know how to be." It is one thing to know what is right and good. It is altogether different, and usually much harder, to want what is right and good. It takes the feelings as well as the thoughts to make a mature Christian, at any age. It is of little importance to decide whether emotion or knowledge is the stronger. It is of great importance to recognize that both are needed. The church, in its efforts at Christian nurture, must seek to use both.

This means that we should lead people of all ages into experiences in which they feel the presence of God. Long ago the young Isaiah went into the Temple. There he worshiped with greater reality and with greater effect than ever before. The experience left him saying to God, "Here am I, Lord, send me." Included in our plans for Christian nurture should be worship experiences that send people of our generation to do the tasks to which God calls them.

We should lead people into experiences in which they confront great souls of the past and present. The young person who comes to know about Albert Schweitzer cannot help but be moved to give something of himself to the work of the Kingdom. Many an American Christian remembers the day he shook the hand of Toyohiko Kagawa. Our plans for Christian nurture should include opportunity to know outstanding Christians of every generation.

We should lead people into experiences in which they confront need and are moved to help meet that need. The clothing, food, and money which Christians give to relieve suffering shows the response of people to real need. The cause that stirs our emotions is sure of our interest and support. Christian nurture should give people of all ages opportunity to work and give to meet the needs of others. This calls for work camps, for service projects, and for sacrificial giving as well as for study.

Everyone learns, and everyone teaches

It is true that the teacher usually knows more and works harder than the pupil. But we have often exaggerated the difference. The teacher, if he is a good teacher, is learning even as he teaches. The work and study which are necessary as he prepares to teach result in learning for him. As he meets with a group, he learns from them. Perhaps he does not learn new truth about the content of what he is teaching, but he learns about people and about living, and that is important.

It is also true that the learner teaches. Sometimes he teaches by the questions he raises or the comments he makes in the class. Sometimes he becomes the teacher later on when he helps someone else find the new truth that came to him in class discussion.

It may seem utterly elementary to make this point about pupil teaching and teacher learning. We need to recognize, however, that the teacher becomes a better teacher and the pupil a better pupil when each realizes that this is true. Someone once put in striking form this idea: "Unless it happens to the teacher, it will not happen to the pupil."

Christian nurture must make use of varied methods

Just as there is no one road that each must travel to mature Christian faith and life, so there is no one method or series of methods which the group leader must use. The method to be used in a given session depends on many things—the purpose of the session, the nature of the lesson or program, the group (age, experience, background, needs), the leader with his special background and abilities. One thing, however, is sure. That is that no one method is good week after week. The leader who is deserving of the trust the church places in him must pay the price of study, prayer, planning, and practice. He must be able to use whatever methods are most likely to further the Christian growth of those with whom he works in the life of the church.

CHAPTER III

Organizing the Church to Serve Families

"Something happens to the members when a local church accepts as its goal a 'family-centered emphasis.' A new vigor and sense of mission are felt. The home, more often than not the object of sentimental utterances, takes on a down-to-earth realism when parents and other church leaders set out in earnest to make the church family-centered. A growing awareness comes that the family circle provides the best opportunity, surpassing even the church, for inculcating the Christian beliefs and teachings in ways resulting in their expression in all relationships of life.

"Only as the church saves the members of families within their own homes can the church hope to save the world." If there are to be in the world more love and less hatred, more understanding and less prejudice, more social concern and less selfishness, more peace and less war, more faith and less fear, then these Christian virtues must first be practiced in family relationships. And the local church as an institution must break from many of its traditional and ecclesiastical practices and patterns in order to transform itself into a family-centered fellowship.

"We must consider the needs of our parents and families first, rather than what has always been a part of the parish program or what should be added to it to make it more like the church down the street. Families need much more help than most churches are giving them in their efforts to gain a knowledge of the Scriptures, an appreciation of the Christian movement through the centuries, and an understanding of the philosophy, content, and method of Christian religious education as it takes place in homes and churches. Parents also need guidance in discovering the great significance and joy of that comradeship which comes only as members of families work and play and worship together."[1]

What Is a Family?

"What is a family? Members of families—as persons—are children of the eternal God and share his nature. The Christian family group is more than a lifelong association of individual believers. The Bible clearly teaches that the family, even as the Church, was instituted by God to serve his purposes and to be responsible to him. The Christian family has a divine mission! This includes the religious nurture of children to full and complete commitment to Christ as their Lord and Savior and to their personal acceptance of the responsibilities of churchmanship. Included also is the family's responsibility for the continuing religious development of adults through middle age and on through old age. This biblical and theological concept of the family is new in Christian education. It lays a fundamental foundation for co-operation between home and church.

"What is a family? Some congregations serve adult households almost exclusively; others minister chiefly to 'young families.' One church found that of 422 families of its membership, 199 had no children living at home! Indeed, in many churches 'childless' homes are the most numerous! Furthermore, there are three-generation families and families of single adults who maintain a home. Families of "adults-only" present opportunities for Christian education that have been overlooked until recently. Only a family life program with much variety can serve all families.

"Families pass through recognizable stages of development and in each stage there is opportunity of further family growth. The newly married couple is confronted by the adjustments of young adult life and beginning marriage. But with the coming of the first baby, life for them undergoes a radical—although thrilling—change. New problems are encountered in rearing children and in adjusting to each other as parents. Then still further challenge faces them as their children grow to and through adolescence. And now today, because of the lengthening life span, families must master the adjustments of later decades of adult life as "retired" parents and with married children.

"If we are to meet such needs and truly enrich family life in the homes of our parishes we must do more than preach about it and

---

[1] Reprinted by permission with some changes and additions from the *International Journal of Religious Education* of October, 1950.

discuss it. We must frankly face our present program—its weakness as well as its strength.

"The particular pattern of organization set up to develop the plans for a family-centered parish program will vary according to local needs and denominational recommendations."[1]

Principles for a Family Life Program

At a national family life conference held by one of the denominations, the following principles for a family life program were developed:

> The family life program is not the entire church program but as an important part of the whole must be planned in relation to the other parts.
>
> The family life program should be planned in co-operation with parents and young people so that it may meet their felt needs.
>
> A family life program should be "tailor-made" to fit the family composition of the local parish. Some ministers report their church membership to be 80 per cent "adult households"; others serve 90 per cent "young families with small children."
>
> The church family program should recognize family services available to families locally and the church's responsibility for participation in the community family life program.
>
> Local church family life programs are most effective when planned to utilize fully denominational resources; curriculum, literature, and leadership.
>
> The family life program has many goals, but the major one is the strengthening of the family itself.
>
> The family life program seeks especially to strengthen the family as a generating center of Christian faith for all members of the family.
>
> A family life program will recognize that family groups may develop as Christian groups through recognizable stages of growth, and it will seek to lead families in lifelong development.[2]

---

[1] From a paper by Richard Lentz; used with his permission.

[2] From the Second National Family Life Conference, The Methodist Church.

Steps of Procedure

Three steps of procedure might be suggested:

One—Find out what helps your own denomination has to offer in developing the church program to stress family-centered activities. A recent study of the literature in this field attempted to gather together what is now available from denominational departments of Christian education. More than 1,400 separate pieces of literature were reviewed and later it was discovered that a number of additional publications had been missed! What your own denomination has developed will probably be most effective in your church.

Two—Discover what the implications are of your present program for family life. Look over the church school literature. Compile a list of all of the activities of your church where families or homes were involved. Interview the leaders of your church school, youth group, and women's groups regarding the contacts with homes that are made by their organizations.

Three—Enlist the participation of parents themselves. The church will not seek to operate on homes but to co-operate with them. Many conferences with parents should be held, and much weight will need to be given to the opinions of family leaders.[1]

Elements of a Family-centered Church

"While all the elements of a family-centered church cannot be described in detail surely the following would be included, no matter what size the church membership: There will be an opportunity for family members of all ages (except the very young) to worship together. The program of Christian nurture will bring parents and church school teachers together regularly for study of and consultation about the contents and methods of effective Christian education. There will be careful guidance of parents in family devotions and fellowship. A regular family forum may be scheduled as a place where ways of enriching home life can be shared and encouraged. Family events will be held regularly at the church, providing training in such family activities as worship, arts and crafts, nature lore, sing-

---

[1] Reprinted with same changes and additions from the *International Journal of Religious Education.*

ing, and games. Guidance needs to be given families in living in democratic fashion, tested and strengthened through the use of such techniques as the family council and the closer fellowship of families in the neighborhood from other races, nations, and creeds."[1]

A Year's Calendar in Parent Education

"One very helpful plan which churches are adopting increasingly is to build a calendar of family life activities. This should be kept simple—at least at the start. One or two activities might be proposed for each month. These activities will be developed and promoted, of course, by the different organizations of the church rather than independently by the special committee on family life. One typical calendar is that suggested by the Department of Adult Work and Family Life of the American Baptist Convention.

JANUARY—Family Open House at the church, held on a Sunday afternoon.

FEBRUARY—Parents' Forum, with guest speaker.

MARCH—Parent-Teacher Meeting, discussing the interpretation of Easter in the home.

APRIL—Stress family attendance at Easter services and plan some program of family significance using audio-visual resources, music, or drama.

MAY—Schedule a Parents' Planning Meeting in which they may discuss the programs in which they are interested.
—Schedule on the first Sunday afternoon of National Family Week a Family Tea at church. At this time arrange an exhibit of pictures for the home, a display of recommended books, family hobby articles and worship centers for home use.

JUNE—Make Children's Day an occasion of significance to all the family. Prepare an exhibit of articles made by the children. Arrange a display of literature and textbooks.
—Hold a meeting with parents to suggest helpful literature and to discuss ways of worshiping as a family during the vacation period.

JULY—Family Festival in the out-of-doors, with picnic supper, games, and worship service.
—Encourage families to attend a family camp during their vacation period.

---

[1] Reprinted with same changes and additions from the *International Journal of Religious Education.*

AUGUST—Suggest spots of historic or religious interest, including denominational camp sites, which families might visit during this period.

SEPTEMBER—Parents' Retreat for the purpose of providing fellowship and of planning a year's program.

OCTOBER—Dedication service in the church for parents and church school workers, held during Christian Education Week.

NOVEMBER—Family-Night-at-Church.

—Festival of the Christian Home, with families bringing food for church institutions and dedicating these.

—Family Thanksgiving dinner at the church during Thanksgiving week.

DECEMBER—Christmas Institute for Parents, on observing Christmas in the home.

—Christmas Family Night, with program that has meaning for the entire family."[1]

---

[1] Reprinted with same changes and additions from the *International Journal of Religious Education.*

CHAPTER IV

Principles of Educational Organization and Administration

The purpose of this chapter is to set forth basic principles in organizing for Christian nurture and in administering the program of Christian nurture. The *organizational* principles stated below are directed primarily toward those responsible for *total church program:* official board members, board of Christian education members, pastors, church school superintendents, directors of Christian education. The *administrative* principles are directed primarily toward those who are charged with guiding the work of specific groups or agencies of the local church: chairmen, officers, and counselors of church groups; superintendents of church school divisions and departments. There is no clear line between these two groups of people. The latter group will be concerned about *organizational* principles when the relationship of one group to another or to the church as a whole is considered. The former group will be concerned about *administrative* principles when church-wide projects are conducted and when group leaders are being trained. It is appropriate, therefore, that both sets of principles be included in this chapter.

No attempt is made here to suggest the kind of organization that a church should establish. Organizational patterns tend to follow denominational lines. The polity of a given denomination suggests a corresponding pattern of organization for Christian nurture for churches of that denomination. The best procedure seems to be to begin with the organizational pattern suggested by the denomination, and to follow the principles given below in adapting that pattern to a particular congregation and in administering the programs of the groups that are established.

Principles of Organization

Organization exists to help the church in its work of developing Christian persons and a Christian society

If any agency begins to serve its own purposes rather than those of the church, it is time to ask whether that agency has a right to exist.

Final responsibility for Christian nurture should be vested in the official body of a church

We have in mind the body variously called official board, consistory, session, vestry, church council. This principle recognizes that the congregation as a whole is responsible for the Christian nurture of its people. Therefore the official body is responsible to see to it that an effective program of Christian nurture is provided.

Planning of educational policy and general supervision of educational program should be assigned to a board or a committee which is responsible to the official body of the church

It is too much to expect that one elected church board will give detailed consideration to the work of all of the programs and agencies of that church. This is especially true of the large church, but it is also true of the small church. There is need for a particular group to oversee the educational work of the church. In most denominations this group is known as the commission, committee, or board of Christian education. In others it bears such a title as program board or program committee.

Organization should bring about unity of program in the church

A good organizational structure requires that each group in the church be clearly related to the church as a whole, through the responsible board or committee. Each group should also be related to the other groups in such a way that they will supplement each other rather than waste effort through duplication.

Organization should secure the fullest participation by individual members of the church, including all age groups

Every member of a church should have the feeling that this is "our church" and that he is an essential part of it. Every time a person thinks of his church as "their church," there is a danger signal. Organization can go a long way toward assuring individual participation. It can see to it that every group is represented in the meetings where policies are made. Each member of the group may have a share in policy-making by giving suggestions to his representative in advance. Each member may be informed about policy through report and discussion afterwards.

When the organizational pattern of a church is charted, it should be possible to follow a line from any member of a church group through to the official body of the church. Information and suggestions should flow *both ways* so each person may feel himself a responsible part of the church.

Organizational structure should be as simple as possible

There should be as many organizations as are needed to get the work of the church done effectively, and no more. There should be as many offices and committees as are needed by the church and its organizations, and no more. Organizations, offices, and committees should continue as long as there is significant work for them to do. If the need no longer exists, let the organization go out of existence. One good rule is to appoint as few standing committees as possible. They tend to perpetuate themselves. Rather, appoint special committees which serve only until they have done their work.

The church can help simplify its organization by arranging for a statement of function for each organization and committee. Such statements of function will clear away a great deal of confusion, and will help church groups to work to advantage. They will also show which organizations have a real place in the life of the church and which serve no real purpose. The church may discover that some important work is not being done and that a new organization is needed or that an existing one should undertake a new purpose.

Practical Steps Toward Unity

The organizational principles which have been listed call for a unified structure in which each church group is related clearly to other groups and to the church as a whole. Time was when such church groups as the Sunday school, the young people's society, the men's group, and the women's group were entirely independent. Each conducted its program with little thought for the program and objectives of the others. That day should be past. In many cases, however, the pattern of independent organizations persists, even though church leaders know that it should not. The question that confronts the administrator, therefore is: How may a church with independent organizations move toward greater unity?

There is no easy answer to this question. The answer for any particular church depends on so many variables that no one course can be mapped out. However, we can offer some suggestions that will help point out the steps that may be taken.

Measure all activities according to their effect on people. Measuring by effect on people rather than by such organizational goals as attendance, membership, and the amount in the treasury will often pave the way toward unity of program and organization.

Check your church against the principles of organization that were listed at the beginning of this chapter. This may suggest points where changes ought to be made.

Provide for regular reports by all church organizations to the bodies to which they are responsible. Such reports may enable your church to make better use of the organizational channels it now has. If the channels are not clear, you will discover that fact and try to change them.

Secure as much family participation as you can. The events in which families participate must fit into the schedules of two or more age groups. These events are likely to have more careful scrutiny than events planned by and for one group alone. The church that serves its families well is on the road to a unified program.

Engage in occasional all-church projects. Such projects, if they are of broad enough interest to appeal to all age groups, will result in some integration, at least for the duration of the project. Projects related to church school curriculum or to special anniversaries in church and community are especially valuable.

Establish councils to serve as clearinghouses for the different age groups in the larger churches. The smaller churches may accomplish the same purposes through informal conversation among a few leaders, or through the official board or board of education.

Move toward unity through the pattern of organization that best fits your own church and the denomination of which you are a part.

Principles of Administration[1]

It is significant that the word "administer" is mostly "minister," and the basic meaning of minister is servant. The administrator of a group or program is, therefore, the servant of that group or program. He is not its autocrat or boss. He does not seek status or position for himself. He helps the group do its best work. Jesus said, "Whoever would be great among you must be your servant." The Christian ideal of service is basic to the task of the church administrator.

Experience has shown that good administration is based on the following principles:

---

[1] These principles are suggested by William F. Case in *A Democratic Conception of the Administration of the Local Church.*

Administration should operate in harmony with the objectives of the church

It is obvious that the program content of a church group may make it easier or harder for the church to accomplish its real purposes. It is not so obvious, but it is true, that the way in which an organization is administered affects the success of that organization in accomplishing its purposes. A church school superintendent may be sincere, conscientious, and competent. However, if he antagonizes people, setting them against each other and against himself, he makes it hard for that church school to get its real job done. Or he may go all out for numbers but ignore quality of program. Again, he may set up a well charted organization and outline an excellent curriculum. But if he pays little attention to the number of people who come, he defeats the purpose of the church school. Then there is the administrator who brings into the church all the procedures of business or of the armed services, without realizing that some of them are foreign to the spirit of the church.

He who would be great among administrators must serve the real purposes of the church in all that he does.

Administration must be flexible, yet stable

The needs of people and the circumstances around them are constantly changing. We are continually finding new ways to understand people and to work with them. The church, like any other agency that deals with people, must adjust to these changes. It is the work of the administrator to keep his agency flexible.

But life is not all change. We inherit lessons and values from the past, and the wise man does not ignore them. This is particularly true of the church. There is the rich background in the Old Testament, the climax in the life and ministry of Jesus, the long, slow development of the church, the fresh insights of the Reformation, the American churches with their new strength, and the younger churches in many lands overseas.

The administrator seeks to blend in the church the strength of heritage and the best insight of new discovery.

Stable administration draws strength not only from time-honored heritage, but from the experience of last year and the last generation.

It keeps records of projects and activities, of meetings and organizations so their experience is not lost. It also conserves the experience of seasoned committee members through overlapping terms of office.

Administration must be concerned about people

We have hinted broadly in this direction several times. Let the administrator show his concern for people in at least two ways. Let him measure the effectiveness of all that he does by the effect on people. Are they becoming more Christian in their understandings and their attitudes? Are they becoming more and more able to act as Christians in their own living, in the life of the church, and in society in general? These questions are more important than the size of enrollment, the average attendance, or the balance in the treasury.

Let the administrator draw as many people as possible into active participation. This calls for more than letting people pass a motion to approve policies which the administrator or the executive committee has worked out. The people should have a share in developing policies, and in deciding how those policies shall be put into effect. If this is done, the resulting policies will probably be better than if they were worked out by a small inner circle. Certainly the policies will be *better accepted* if many people have had a share in their development.

Besides, more people will have grown to understand the organization and to have a real desire for its success. Would that we could say this kind of democratic administration can be handled quickly. Time is a price we must pay for democratic administration, but the results are worth it!

Administration performs a series of functions

These functions form a cycle through which every effective group must go. We will list seven such functions. Failures in church groups can usually be traced to poor work in one or more of these seven functions.

Planning

This involves formulating purposes and arriving at means by which these purposes may be achieved. Church groups are often weak at this point, for we assume that everybody knows the purpose of the church and its organizations. But not everybody knows the purpose of every organization in the church. It is difficult for a group to plan the way it will achieve a purpose if that purpose is a hazy blur in the minds of its people.

Knowing that this is so, some administrators do the planning themselves. The results may look good on paper, but they are seldom good in individual and group experience. Let planning be a shared experience.

Organizing

Be sure that the organization needed to carry out the plans is provided. So far as possible use the organization that already exists. Where it is lacking or inadequate, take steps to change it. Responsibility for organization includes responsibility for providing the necessary personnel, equipment, and finances. Delegation of responsibility is essential here. The good administrator does not try to do it all himself.

Executing

See that the plans are actually carried out. This must be done thoroughly, so the work is completed rather than allowed to dangle indefinitely in a half-finished condition. It must be done effectively, so people feel they are part of a "going concern."

Supervising

It is not enough to start the wheels of organization going and then assume that the plans will be well executed. Someone must supervise the process. This includes coaching or training workers so they understand what they are to do and how they are to do it. It includes keeping up the morale of workers. It means revising the plans if they prove faulty. A specific administrator may delegate the function rather than perform it himself. The responsibility to see that there is supervision, however, belongs to the administrator.

Co-ordinating

The various activities of a group need to be co-ordinated so that they result in a unified program. The activities of the various groups in a church need to be co-ordinated so they support each other as parts of the same church. The need here is for proper communication. The larger the church, the more definite must be the provision for this communication. It may take place in the official board, in a cabinet created as a clearinghouse, in informal conversation after the morning worship service, or even on the golf course, at an informal luncheon, or on the way home from work.

Publicizing

We have a great deal to learn about interpreting the program of the church so people will understand and support it. A later chapter is devoted to this subject, but mention must be made of it here for it is an important function of the administrator.

Evaluating

Any church group needs to see what it has done, and how well. Too often we have assumed that whatever is done by a church group is good. Perhaps it is, but is it good enough? We will not carry this subject further, for a chapter is devoted to it.

Evaluation will almost always lead to further planning. So the cycle goes on. If administration is sound, the work of the group improves steadily, and the figure is that of the spiral rather than that of the cycle. There is no stopping place in administration. The ultimate goals are far off. Our efforts are insufficient, but our gains hold promise and they give us hope. Like Paul and Apollos, we are "fellow workmen for God" who is both our goal and our aid.

CHAPTER V

Building the Program

The program of the church or of any group in the church is good if it helps in the Christian nurture of the people who make up the church and who are members of its groups. The program of the church or of a church group is not good whenever it fails to contribute to Christian nurture. To build a program which serves the needs of people and of church groups is far from easy. Each group is different from every other, and the individuals within a group are different. In fact, a particular person or group will seldom be the same from one meeting to the next. Truly, the way of the program builder is hard. What can we say to help him?

Characteristics of an Effective Program

It may be helpful in building or evaluating the program of Christian nurture in a church to check that program against characteristics that are generally found in effective efforts at Christian nurture. The following eighteen characteristics are offered for this purpose.

> It is based upon a clearly defined statement of purpose which is consistent with the Christian faith.
>
> It recognizes man as a child of God who is "a little lower than the angels" and also a sinful creature who needs redemption.
>
> It recognizes the presence of the Holy Spirit and of his power to regenerate men and to bring about a progressive and continuous development of Christian character.
>
> The content of the curriculum and the whole experience of Christian education must have a sound theological grounding and must be centered in the gospel with its promises and its demands.

It relates the Christian gospel to all of the needs and developmental tasks of growing individuals.

It appeals to and brings about desirable changes in the emotional life of the individual as well as in his intellectual concepts.

It is aware of the problems within the life of the community and conscious of its responsibility for community affairs.

It recognizes the home as the basic agency for Christian nurture.

It provides guidance to enable the home to be a true school for Christian living.

It supplements the teaching of the home through the church's teaching agencies, recognizing sound principles of grading and grouping.

It reaches every individual and group within the congregation.

It has an effective outreach to those outside the Christian church.

It utilizes sound educational principles and procedures.

It avails itself of all resources that can contribute to Christian growth, particularly the Bible, devotional materials, art, the history of the Christian church.

It gives opportunity through programs, projects, and other means for developing attitudes, acts, and habits that are in harmony with the spirit and teachings of Christ.

It discovers and uses community resources.

It co-operates with other character-building agencies of the community, and with denominational and interdenominational church agencies.

It promotes Christian fellowship in the deepest sense of that term.

What Shall Be Included in the Program of the Church?

Other publications list many types of activities and enterprises for inclusion in the program for the Christian education of children, young people, and adults. These need not be repeated here, but there is need for a general outline of the types of elements that are essential to any well rounded church program.

Instruction

The word, "instruction," is a red flag to some educators because of the stereotyped, mechanical, unsound ways in which instruction too often has been carried on. Here, however, it is used to refer to the process of helping persons learn important facts, with the learning of those facts as the immediate and definite, although not usually the ultimate objective. There are some things to be learned which cannot be left to chance, or be made simply incidental to the various activities in which individuals and groups may engage. Those who would have knowledge gained only in bits and only when some ongoing activity is blocked by lack of it, slight the importance of large bodies of knowledge and make education but an atomistic process that will not hang together. It is recognized, of course, that instruction should be carried on on the basis of the very best and most effective procedures; that learning should not be thought of as a submissive, passive absorption of the dictatorial utterings of a teacher; and that forward steps should begin where the learner is and continue under a maximum of self-propulsion. But this recognition must not be allowed to minimize the importance of mastering definite areas of knowledge.

The fullest Christian lives are those which are lived in light of a clear understanding of the great currents which have swept through history, of the development of religious conceptions, of the history of Christian thinking and Christian institutions. Persons with such understanding are best able to interpret the present, to make their own lives fruitful, and to see in the mirror of the present and the past a vision of the years ahead. So also can they recognize the evil and the good in the present, distinguish between the temporary and the permanent, and "prove all things," holding fast "that which is good." The church should not neglect the importance of facts, of definite bodies of knowledge.

The church program should include opportunities for the gaining of at least six types of information.

Knowledge of God and of Jesus

To know God and Jesus is essential to Christian living. Complete knowledge, understanding, and appreciation will not come simply by studying about them, but neither will it come without careful studying. It is important to know the revelations of God that have been given to men, and to know the life and teachings of Jesus. Opportunities for gaining this knowledge should be included in the program of the church.

Knowledge of the Bible and of other religious history and literature

Enrichment of life as well as guidance for living can be found in the history of religions and religious institutions and in the literature produced by them. For Christians the Bible stands out pre-eminently.

Knowledge of the Christian Church

Unless a Christian knows the history of the movement of which he is a part, he is in no position to exert a positive influence upon its future. On the negative side, knowledge of church history can help prevent the repetition of ancient mistakes.

Knowledge of biography

One of the very best ways to become an intelligent, effective Christian is to steep oneself in the records of the great lives of history. Even through the printed page these lives radiate a penetrating light which has great power to illumine and inspire.

Knowledge of other peoples

Christian living involves association with others. Moreover, no part of the life of this world can be lifted to adequate heights unless all other parts are also lifted. Hence, knowledge and sympathetic understanding of other peoples is necessary.

Knowledge of current social life and problems

Here is an item that needs to be stressed, not because it exceeds the previous items in importance, but because the church has so largely neglected it. Before any improvement whatever of social systems, institutions, practices, and organizations can be brought about, there must be an understanding of them, and that understanding needs to be in the full light of Christian ideals. Every group, young or old, should be guided to the extent of its ability to a knowledge of current social problems. Even the beginners can and should be helped to recognize that the necessity for bringing gifts for some poor child of the neighborhood rests back upon something wrong with the way people live together. If all along the line of development, children, young people, and adults are led to a keen sense of the problems in current situations in the immediate community and beyond, there will be more action—and more intelligent action—in the direction of changing what is to something that is better.

For the church to deal with many of the great social issues is such a delicate matter that two cautions should be observed.

In the first place, in trying to lead its constituents to an awareness of the issues and what they involve, it should be sure to use the educational method. This means that the process will be gradual, and will take into account the present attitudes and prejudices of all persons involved. The leaders will not undertake to force conclusions, but will move toward conclusions in a democratic way; in fact, they may leave the question of conclusions entirely to individual judgment.

This may mean that the church will have to make careful plans to develop the ability of its constituents to carry on group thinking. The fact is that few church groups manifest this ability in any large degree. Adults in particular are accustomed to being told; and if the telling is too frequently out of harmony with deep seated prejudices and points of view, the teller loses his opportunity to tell. Possibly there will be required a basic change in our churches if the educational approach is to be used in studying social issues. The preacher cannot and ought not to pretend to speak for a whole congregation, unless that congregation has done some thinking and has formulated its point of view. But entirely apart from any attempt to represent his congregation, the pastor cannot depend exclusively upon sermons to change attitudes or to stimulate new thinking. Individuals and groups must be led through analysis of problems, search for facts, exchange of opinion and experience, and other steps involved in a complete educative process. The change from the usual procedure to this procedure will come slowly in most churches, but it is important enough to warrant the necessary effort.

The second caution is that there should be an insistence upon getting facts. Old prejudices may be replaced by new prejudices by means of emotional appeals, or other devices, but substantial and significant changes in thinking must be based upon knowledge. Such social problems as the church faces today are complicated; they do not permit of easy solution. To deal with them at all requires the persistence of genuine truth-seeking. That church which is not willing to seek facts should not deal with social issues; but, if it does not deal with social issues, it is failing in its obligation.

Worship

If the church omits worship from its program, it neglects that which primarily distinguishes it from other agencies. Fellowship with God and with fellow men reaches its highest peaks in worship. Worship is essential to religious living.

In general it may be said that there are two kinds of worship; that which is consciously planned and participated in somewhat as an experience by itself, and that which is a sort of "overtone" in the on-going activities of life. Many persons never feel that they are worshiping except during a service labeled devotions or worship. A few have an almost constant sense of the presence of God and consequently of fellowship with him. The program of the church should foster both types of experience.

It is exceedingly important to note that there cannot be fellowship with God in the Christian sense unless a person is striving to live a righteous life. Let anyone draw permanently apart from the world and within himself, and his worship will become empty. This suggests that the worship opportunities and the training for worship provided by the church should be specifically related to the experiences of life. In this way the discouragements, failures, aspirations, ideals, and plans of individuals, and the problems and achievements of society will be viewed with something of the perspective of God and will be seen in their universal rather than only in their immediate relationships. It is impossible to believe that when Jesus went apart to pray he left behind him all thought of what he had been doing; rather, he seems to have reviewed his work with God. His reason for getting away probably was not to escape from his task but to escape from the little things that he might see the large ones, and to escape from the large ones that he might appreciate the little ones. Worship in the church should be such that through it persons can face life with God and bring unity and strength out of weakness and confusion. It should help the worshipers to "see life steadily and see it whole," but nevertheless to *see life.*

Well planned worship will take into account the experiences of life. Often the themes for specific services can be based upon some important event or experience or condition that is common to the members of the worshiping group. Perhaps there has been some community, national, or world crisis; some joyous experience; or the initiation of some great project which has concerned the group as a whole.

Moreover, each individual is constantly having various experiences. The common elements in all these will be caught up in the service of worship, will be examined in fellowship with God, and evaluated in terms of the ideals of God for mankind. Then there will be renewed consecration to the will of God, and the worshipers will be sent forth as changed persons who will themselves make changes in certain aspects of the life of their community and the world. Worship at its best is not something apart from life; it is a part of life. The effective church carefully provides for training in worship and for the experience of vital worship.

Participation in improving society

The function of the church in relation to the individual has been comparatively clear. The church has felt responsible for developing what is thought of as individual Christian character, for leading the individual to God, for bringing courage, fortitude, faith, and love into each person's life. But the function of the church in relation to social patterns, organizations, systems, and institutions has not been so clear. The objectives of the church should point in the direction both of the individual and of the social order. That much may be widely accepted. But what shall be the program of the church for the improvement of the social order? This is a difficult question, but a few suggestions can be offered.

In thinking of the function of the church in relation to the social order, it should be kept in mind that the church is an institution. As such it naturally tends to conserve the past. This it ought to do, and this must continue to be an important function, even though it is inevitable that in this conservation there will be included some things that are outworn and undesirable as well as much that has permanent value. The church must fulfill the function of the priest, which is to codify, preserve, and pass on the finest that is revealed by the prophet and by the experience of the race. This fact must not be forgotten.

There are several possible ways for the church to participate in improving the social order. The study of current social issues as a part of the church program was discussed previously in this chapter and is *basic to the four procedures mentioned here*—procedures which go beyond the point of study.

a. The church can urge its constituents to be active in civic relations. In doing this it need not express any preferences as to the channels through which to work, but may simply keep before its people the fact that as professing Christians they have peculiar responsibilities as citizens. The studying and group thinking suggested earlier in this chapter should aid each person in deciding what goals to seek and through what extra-church channels to work.

b. The church can urge its young people to prepare for public service. In doing this, it may well help these young people to understand the difficulties in politics and government, and the temptations to undesirable compromises and even to dishonesty. In doing so, it will fortify the future leaders of government in a way not possible by means of abstract ideals.

c. The church can sometimes give expression to the judgment of its constituents on important social issues.

While an important function of the church is, with the priest, to conserve the values that have come out of the past, it must also fulfill the function of the prophet. Its voice will be heard much further than will the voice of any individual prophet, and its influence can be greater. It should be the conscience for society. Too often in the past it has followed, or at least has been some distance behind the leaders of the procession for righteousness. The church ought to be more nearly in the lead than it sometimes is.

Whenever the church does propose to take definite positions on social questions, it should be sure that it is dealing with *major moral* issues. For it to attack every minor question that may arise will be to dissipate its energies and drown its voice by much speaking. And if it speaks with reference to any except those issues which are clearly moral in character, it will be stepping aside from its primary function. Of course, there are differences of opinion as to just what questions involve moral issues. But the church can be careful to keep its attention centered on *the welfare of persons* in the more important aspects of living.

Furthermore, it must not undertake to choose from among solutions which do not differ essentially with reference to their moral character. For example, it should not undertake to determine the details of taxation policies, but if existing taxing policies place heavier burdens upon those unable to pay than upon the well-to-do, thus making the poor the victims of oppression, it may become the business of the church to speak. While there is a degree of truth in the contention that the church should keep out of business, the church cannot escape its obligation to oppose those policies of business and government which in a major degree are sins against the ideals of the Fatherhood of God and the brotherhood of man. For it to study war and its causes and cure, or the competitive versus the co-operative philosophy of society, or the effect of alcohol upon society, is legitimate because each is a major question and each should be settled on the basis of Christian ideals.

d. The church may sometimes take definite action designed to bring about specific changes in organized society. Suppose that the members of a certain church have carefully studied the problems of war and have come to the conclusion that there should not be military training in high schools. Suppose, also, that the high school in the community includes military training in its curriculum. What can the church do about it, more than to express an opinion and urge its members to work through extra-church channels to change the situation?

For one thing, it can launch a campaign to get the voters to require the board of education to change its policy. Such a campaign, of course, should be carried on according to the very highest principles, but it can be aggressive and persistent. Certainly, there may be reactions against the church because of this activity, but if the church has reached the clear conviction that military training in the high school is, in its results, basically inconsistent with Christian principles, it is justified in moving forward; in fact, it would be unjustified in doing otherwise. There are some issues on which the church must speak by more than resolutions, or its resolutions will be mere lip service.

Fellowship

There are some needs which can be met only by active, guided participation in group life. Three such needs are mentioned here.

First, everyone needs skill in adjusting himself to other persons. Unless he is a recluse, he frequently will be rubbing elbows with his fellows. He cannot expect to force them into his own pattern of living and so he must know how to adjust himself to them. The little child must learn to wait his turn for the scissors when the children in his group are making posters. The adolescent must learn how to avoid being ostracized from worth-while friendships. The adult must be able to dwell in peace and harmony with his next-door neighbor. The program of the church should provide for gaining these and similar skills.

A second illustration is the need for personal integrity. Thoroughgoing honesty with one's fellow men is a rare quality. All persons need the ability to face difficulties without building false alibis, the ability to evaluate others on the basis of facts rather than prejudices, and the ability to admit their own shortcomings in their social contacts. Honesty is not merely a matter of keeping hands off one's neighbor's automobile. It has many ramifications and aspects. It can be developed through guided participation in group life.

Third, for the sake of abundant living, persons need opportunities just to enjoy other persons. Such enjoyment enlarges fellowship, and provision for it should be included in the program of the church.

These, then—instruction, worship, participation in improving society, and fellowship—are four major phases of the total program of the church, the total program of Christian education. Although they are presented separately here, they are interrelated, and they overlap. Any one of them is dependent upon the others, and all should be carried forward as a unified whole.

In the very nature of the situation, the concerns of the local church ought to move beyond itself. In the past it has been too largely centered upon its own maintenance as an institution, and has been too insistent that those who are to be served by it must come within the doors of its building. It ought to exist as a means to an end, not as an end in itself. It should reach out into homes where great needs exist and tremendous possibilities may be found; into the life of the community, the influence of which is often subtle but always powerful; into the world at large, where sinister forces too often govern the lives of men. The business of the church is to bring men into right relations to themselves, to their fellows, and to God. Its program must be constructed to this end, not for the sake of its own glorification.

Steps in Program Building

It is one thing to recognize the general marks of a good program. It is an altogether different matter to be able to work with a church and its groups in planning a program that will look good on paper and will also be good! Not even the wisest of counsel on the printed page can guarantee a good program. It takes wise counsel, incarnate in a skillful and consecrated leader and in an equally skillful and consecrated group to do that. Experience gained in a large number of efforts at program planning has shown that certain steps are essential to it. This is particularly true if the church wishes to practice the sound advice of drawing as many people as possible into the planning process. A five-step process is offered here, centering in a planning retreat.[1]

Advance planning in the various church groups

Invite the various groups of the church to help prepare for a planning retreat. Ask each of them to evaluate the present program of the church. What is good about it, and why? What needs related to Chris-

[1] Adapted from the steps suggested by William F. Case in *A Democratic Conception of the Administration of the Local Church.*

tian nurture are not now being met? How effective is the impact of the church on the community? How adequate is the program for all age groups and all interest groups?

Ask each group then to think of its own members, their interests and needs. Let each member ask himself what he would most like to discuss, what it is that concerns him most, what he wishes the church would do for him. What difficulties do members of this group face in the community? What opportunities do they wish the community would provide?

Let each group then make specific program suggestions, in view of its evaluation and in view of the wishes and needs of individual members. The group should appoint someone to bring these suggestions into the planning retreat at the appropriate time.

A program planning retreat

Invite the total membership of the church, if practicable, to a program-planning retreat. In large churches include leaders and representative members of all church groups. Do not limit the retreat to a small inner circle. Schedule the retreat for a time when most members will be free to attend and when there will be time for unhurried discussion. Choose a place for the retreat that is close, but not too close! A camp or conference ground is a good place if there is one within reach. Some churches reserve an entire Sunday for the retreat. A Sunday in late spring or early summer is good, for it leaves time for necessary follow-up before fall.

The retreat program will include worship, reports, discussion, and fellowship. If the retreat is held on Sunday, the worship period will take the place of the usual Sunday worship service. Let it not be a routine service, however, but one which stimulates the members to give themselves to planning a program that will fulfill the role of the church and meet the needs of people.

Reports of evaluation and program suggestions from the various church groups will be given, with opportunity for some questions and discussion. The group will then proceed to sift out the suggestions, approving those that seem good and disapproving or amending others. One helpful procedure, especially in the larger church, is to divide the members into small groups of six to ten for discussion of the various suggestions. In small groups, everyone feels free to participate. Suggestions are weighed on their merits. When these groups report back to the entire retreat body it is possible to settle rather easily on the ideas that merit a place in the program.

Fellowship should be encouraged. In the large church, the newly organized church, or the church with many new members, the fellowship period gives people a chance to become acquainted. Regardless of the nature of the group it is well to give people a period of refreshment during a retreat. Weary bodies seldom house good ideas.

Committee delegated to work out tentative program

The planning retreat should reach agreement on program suggestions. It can scarcely be expected to put those suggestions into form for final adoption. This requires a small group that can choose phrases, check dates, and build a program calendar. This committee should do its work during the summer and be prepared to make its report in early fall.

How shall this committee be made up? If the church organization includes a board or committee to which this task may be delegated, fine! In some cases the official board may be able and willing to take this assignment. More often, the board or committee on Christian education may do it. If the church has a program board or committee, this group is a natural. Sometimes it will be preferable for the retreat itself or the official board to appoint a special planning committee for this one function.

Adoption of the program

At an appropriate time, preferably in early fall, the planning committee submits its report to the total membership in a church-wide meeting. The report should be duplicated so that each person may have a copy. Otherwise a program will be considered on the basis of what members can recall from hearing the report read, and the result will satisfy no one. If this meeting includes many who were not in the retreat, it may be well again to divide into small groups for discussion in which all may participate.

Putting the program into effect

Following adoption of a program, the person or group responsible for each element of it proceeds to put it into effect. The functions of administration that were listed in Chapter 4 will guide these people in putting into effect the agreements reached by the group as a whole.

Two results follow this kind of planning that are more difficult to achieve if the planning is done by only a chosen few. One is wide acceptance of the plan and participation in it. If we have shared in building a program, we want to have a share in putting it into practice. Promotion is much easier when there has been democratic planning.

The other result that follows naturally is increased co-operation. The kind of planning we have described means that each group is informed about what the others will do. Duplications and conflicts can be avoided. Co-operation is made natural where two or more groups have common concerns. The preacher, for example, can use his preaching program to strengthen the entire work of the church when he and his people have decided together what they will try to accomplish.

Some Special Concerns of the Program Builder

These five steps in program building have been tested by experience and are sound. By themselves, however, they are not a cure-all for the ills of a church program. He who would take these five steps successfully must give attention to a number of special concerns that will help to develop a successful program.

Determining objectives

How can a local church set up sound objectives? These objectives must be consistent with the purpose of the Christian Church as a whole. They must be suited to the people of the particular church with their special needs and abilities. There is no rule of thumb that will give us sound objectives for every church, but we believe these five suggestions will help.

Adopt, or adapt, a general statement of objectives for the church. The objectives stated in Chapter 1 will be of help in defining the objectives of the local church. Most churches will find them a good statement of the purposes they ought to achieve. This kind of statement will not help very much in helping a teacher plan his work from week to week, but it will help him keep his over-all sense of direction.

Adopt, or adapt, a program of work leading step by step toward these objectives. Many denominations are prepared to offer suggestions for such a program to their churches. It may be called a standard, or an achievement plan, or a guide. It is not to be followed slavishly, but it will help a congregation to move forward. This kind of plan usually includes short-term goals for six months or a year as well as long-range goals for a period of years. If your denomination does not have such a program, you will find some of the materials of the National Council of Churches helpful in setting up your own. Also, you might use the program suggested for a denomination organized somewhat like yours.

Encourage groups within the church to rate themselves and to set goals for their future work. Some of these goals should be quantitative, in terms of enrollment, attendance, contributions. Some of these goals should be qualitative, in terms of comprehensive program, service given, and the like.

Set up objectives for each session and each unit of work or program. This suggestion is particularly suited to church school teachers and to leaders of fellowship groups in the church. Curriculum materials usually suggest aims for an individual session or for a series of related sessions. Let the leader adapt these printed aims to the particular group and then work toward them.

The group that works along such lines as these will find that objectives become less academic and forbidding. Rather he will find them helpful in planning and in deciding whether the group is "getting somewhere."

Planning curriculum and selecting materials

Curriculum is one of the words that we use in different ways. "In the broad sense it has been defined as experience under guidance toward the fulfillment of the purposes of Christian education. Whereas the total experience of the individual is certainly educative in the sense that he is learning from life at every moment, all of this complex of situations is not thought of as curriculum. In other words, the curriculum is not the entire social situation within which the person acts and with which he is interacting, but rather that part of it which is consciously planned to attain certain objectives, to realize certain purposes of Christian education."[1]

In its limited sense, curriculum refers to the tools, resources, or materials prepared for use in church school and other organized groups within the church. Curriculum materials include such resources as quarterlies, books, pictures, maps, films, and filmstrips.

A major problem is the selection of the basic materials to be used in the class or group. The following principles will be helpful.

Let printed curriculum materials be selected or approved by a responsible body, probably the board of Christian education.

Be sure that the material is basically Christian, and in harmony with the purposes and program of the local church.

Review the material prepared or recommended by the denomination. This material has been prepared with care, and is likely to include the various emphases that you will want. This material is more likely than any other curriculum series to fit a given church. It is based on the his-

---

[1] *A Guide for Curriculum in Christian Education*—published by the Division of Christian Education of the National Council of Churches—1955. Used by permission.

tory, polity, theology, and program of the denomination to which that church belongs. Illustrations, projects, missionary enterprises, and special programs of that denomination are written into the curriculum material. The projects that a church school class may carry on are part of the program with which the church as a whole is concerned.

Give youth and adult groups a voice in selection. In all cases, however, clear these choices with the responsible body mentioned above.

Be sure that there is continuity from one age group or department to another. This usually means that one curriculum series only should be used in a church school, at least through the senior high department. A chopped-up curriculum means chopped-up experience for children and youth.[1]

Selection of good curriculum material should be followed by interpretation of it so that members of groups, parents, and teachers understand and accept it. This is especially important if a new series is introduced. Move slowly in interpreting a new curriculum series. Take advantage of meetings in which denominational workers present the new materials and point out their values. Get the reactions and suggestions of teachers before final selection is made. Provide help for teachers that they may be able to use the new materials and to gain the values that are inherent in them. Be sure that parents as well as teachers understand the changes that are being considered.

The need for interpretation of curriculum is a constant one. Many churches have learned to their sorrow the folly of stopping their efforts at interpretation when the selection was made. Teachers and parents must be "kept sold." This is important, for it is not easy to learn to use a new series of material. It may seem much simpler to go back to the old and the familiar. And some churches have gone back! When that happens it is much harder to "resell" a group than it was the first time.

A meeting of workers, shortly before the beginning of each new unit or quarter, is practically a must. It gives workers a chance to plan together for their use of the new unit. It requires them to become familiar with it. If there are questions, or difficulties, or differences of opinion, here is the time to work them out. There is some experience which suggests that neighboring churches using the same curriculum materials may well have joint conferences before beginning new units. In such joint conferences they pool their leadership and their ideas. All of the co-operating churches become the gainers, especially the smaller ones.

---

[1] For further suggestions about curriculum selection see Chapter 4 of *A Guide for Curriculum in Christian Education*—published by the Division of Christian Education of the National Council of Churches.

Using audio-visuals

Mixed reactions greet audio-visuals in the church. To some they are the new miracle element in church work. They are the answer! We greet them with open arms. To others they are strange and new, require equipment that is expensive and difficult to operate, and are to be met with suspicion. Neither view is correct. Remember that audio-visuals include nonprojected materials that are easily available, as well as projected materials.

Audio-visuals are not entirely new. We have used charts, maps, blackboards, and posters for many years. Recordings are not new either, though we are finding new ways of using them. Projected pictures, radio, and television are newer. It is only recently that we have had the facilities to make good use of these media in the church.

The administrator will do well to keep in mind such principles as the following in the church use of audio-visuals.

Determine first the purpose to be accomplished in your session or program. It is rarely good to show a picture just for the sake of showing a picture.

Select the type of presentation to be used. Will a motion picture or a filmstrip best serve your purpose? Is a visit possible? It is better to visit a Jewish synagogue than to see pictures of one.

If an audio-visual is chosen select the specific title. Curriculum materials often contain suggestions. Lists of projected audio-visuals which have been evaluated are available from your denomination or from the National Council of Churches.

Arrange for the material. Do this early—from three to six months in advance for seasonal material.

Plan how to use the audio-visual. This includes pre-view by the leader and careful planning of the session in which an audio-visual is to be used. If a guide is available, consider its suggestions.

Prepare the room. Set up the equipment that will be needed, and try it out. Arrange seating for good viewing. Check lighting, darkening facilities, and ventilation.

Prepare the group. Help them to know the kind of material that is being used, the purpose of its use, and the way in which they are expected to participate.

Present the audio-visual, using good technique. Do not let mechanical difficulties get in the way!

Follow through. Secure group participation in discussion and in such planning and activity as is necessary if the purpose is to be achieved. This will include testing or evaluation to enable leader and group to know how well the purpose has been accomplished.

Special days and seasons

Special days and seasons are good if they help the church in the Christian nurture of people. They are bad if they are burdens to the program builder and interruptions to the program. They are of four kinds, so far as church program is concerned: 1) days of special religious significance like Easter and Christmas; 2) promotional days, emphases, and seasons such as Christian Education Week, Youth Week, National Family Week, Children's Day, stewardship and mission emphases; 3) general holidays which are in the minds of all people, for example, Memorial Day and Washington's Birthday; 4) special-interest days which are promoted by particular religious or secular groups. Flag Day and Arbor Day are illustrations.

The days of special religious significance we naturally include in our program each year. We do not merely observe these days but devote some time leading up to them.

Promotional days and seasons are important for the church at large. They are also important to the local church, but there is danger that they may crowd out real program development. The spiritual welfare of people is more important to a church than the annual observance of a given number of emphases. Let the program builder therefore keep these observances in mind. Let him build them into the program wherever feasible. Where it is not feasible to give them major place, let him recognize them through choice of hymns, through appropriate material in bulletins and newsletters, and in similar ways which call attention to them without disrupting program.

General holidays should be recognized where appropriate, but should seldom receive major place in the program of the church.

Special-interest days ought to be recognized according to the need of people for them and according to their relation to the church program. A good guide is to recognize only those that are listed in the denominational calendar of the pastor's plan book and those that have special local meaning.

Resource persons

Resource persons are often like "acres of diamonds"—not appreciated because they are so close we fail to see their value. The program can be greatly enriched by planned use of the special knowledge and experience of the furloughed or returned missionary, the serviceman who has visited the part of the world about which we may be studying, the physician, the artist, the engineer, the craftsman, the teacher who may have just the skill our program needs. The personnel committee of the church might well keep a file of resource persons and the types of contribution each is equipped to make.

Calendarizing the program

A calendar is at least as good for program building as it is for advertising. At least annually, the church should prepare a calendar of events for the information of its people. Such a calendar protects scheduled meetings, avoids conflicts, and encourages attendance.

For each group in the church (and even for each group leader or officer) a calendar showing events and responsibilities is helpful. This specific calendar lists not only the dates of scheduled events, but the times when preparation or follow-up should take place. How much spiritual energy has been lost because preparation and announcement for meetings were begun too late and because follow-up was forgotten! The program calendar encourages a balanced program and enables us to make each program activity more significant. Therefore, calendarize!

More Time for Christian Nurture

Christian educators have often complained about the little time available for their work. What can be done in one short hour a week? This is a legitimate complaint, but we ought to make it a challenge before we make it a complaint.

In planning the program, let us first make good use of the time we do have. If there is an hour, let us plan its use so well that it will be an unforgettable hour! However, the church that does its planning in the manner which we have suggested will find that hour all too short. There are many ways in which additional time can be had. Let us look at a few of them.

The *expanded session* provides an additional period, either on Sunday morning or during the week for the varied program that cannot be crowded into one hour. The *vacation church school* adds intensive programs for several weeks in the summer. The *weekday church school* adds an hour during one of the regular school days for the teaching of religion. Programs like those of scouting, day camps, summer camps, and conferences are all ways of supplementing the time available on Sunday for Christian nurture. Each of these can greatly strengthen the teaching work of the church, especially if it is related to the Sunday program.

Use of the Mass Media of Communication

Newspapers, radio, and television are big business. They influence church people whether we like it or not. Some of this influence is good and some is not. By and large, these media are controlled by private enterprise. There is a measure of governmental control, however, and these enterprises are responsive to the pressure of public opinion. The sensible thing for the church to do is to recognize these facts and then do all it can to influence these media to become positive factors in Christian nurture. How may this be done? These pages are not the place for detailed treatment, but they can suggest directions.

The church may work in at least three ways to affect the influence of these media on the mass of our people. 1) It may help people to know which are the better programs and encourage them to see and hear these. Printed evaluations of programs and features, together with occasional discussion of them in church and community groups will help. Many people will choose the good program even if they have a choice and if they are given information. This works even with comic books! 2) Use good programs and materials in church groups. The youth group that watches a stimulating television program and then discusses it is an illustration. The church school class that uses an appropriate feature story as supplementary material in its class session is another. 3) Bring pressure to bear on publishers, producers, and distributors. Pressure may be good, but be sure that it is sincere and well considered. Let the church not be the tool of special interest!

The church not only influences the general use of these media, but it employs them directly in its own work. We shall not deal here with the content of programs the church may produce, or with techniques it should employ. It is sufficient to express two general principles which churches should follow.

Use the mass media in the interests of the church at large rather than narrowly in the interests of a particular church

Religious emphases in newspaper, radio, and television should cause the general public to be better informed about religion and more favorable to it. Competing church programs are not likely to have this result. The churches, therefore, should work together through a council of churches, federation of churches, or ministerial association. If there is no such interdenominational group, and if there is little chance of getting one, a church may well produce its own programs. Even so, the program should seek to develop an informed and interested public rather than to promote a single church.

Let the technical standards of church productions be at least as high as those of commercially sponsored programs

Helpful suggestions will be found in the book by Clayton Griswold and Charles Schmitz: *Broadcasting Religion,* published by the National Council of Churches.

Special Factors That Affect Program Building

The program that grows out of the kind of process we have described is at the mercy of a good many elements that are beyond the control of any committee. The church cannot control these factors, but it can and should keep them in mind.

One such factor is population change. During the depression years of the thirties, the birth rate fell. During the forties and fifties the birth rate rose sharply. At the same time, improvements in sanitation and medical discoveries have increased the span of life and raised the number of older people. In one age-range, therefore, the church must expect its groups to be relatively small. In the younger and older age-ranges the groups will be larger. From year to year the wave of increase moves up. Population change does not operate at the same rate everywhere. One community is growing rapidly because people are moving in to work in new industry. Another community loses population because its industry is in a period of decline.

What can the church do? It can prepare for the wave of increase by expanding its program and enlarging its building. To do this, however, takes time, planning, and money. In the meantime, how may it best serve the people who overcrowd its rooms? The two- or even three-session plan is one of the best answers. It may be set up on any one of a number of patterns, depending on such factors as the distance people must travel, the relative size of different age-groups, and especially on the number and location of church rooms. One pattern is to hold two church school periods and one worship service. Another is to hold two or three church school sessions and two worship services. A third is to have church school for the younger departments at the same time as the worship service. When this pattern is followed, children may well come into the sanctuary for the early part of the worship service. In any of these patterns the church may serve more people by using its rooms for more than one group on a Sunday.

We are an increasingly mobile population. Church program is especially affected by vacation and week-end mobility. No one is quite sure what the answer is, so far as the church is concerned. The wisest counsel seems to be realism. Get the facts and face them. Some interpret this counsel to mean retrenchment. Shorten the summer Sunday schedule; move it to early morning; reduce to a skeleton schedule; close down altogether during the summer. In most communities, this is not what realism dictates. Realism tells us to serve the people who are at home. Usually there are enough people to justify a good program. Attendance in many churches suffers more from those who stay at home in summer because "nothing happens anyway" than from those who have actually gone out of town. Then, too, mobility may bring people to your community as well as take them away. How can your church serve these visitors? Realism counsels us to make the program and schedule as convenient as possible to our people, and then conduct the kind of program that appeals to those who are within reach.

The nature of the community and of the church membership has a bearing on program. What will work in one church may not work in another. What appeals to the people of one church will not necessarily appeal to those in another. This diversity creates problems for the group that wants to adopt a program planned elsewhere and make it work. However, the church that plans democratically a program designed for its people will naturally develop the kind of church that nurtures its own people as Christians.

CHAPTER VI

Enlisting and Developing Volunteer Workers

One of the most glorious chapters in the story of protestantism is the contribution that volunteer workers have made. A new day for the layman dawned when the doctrine of the priesthood of all believers was accepted. This doctrine says that each man is his own priest and needs no one to be his representative to God. It also says that each man has a measure of responsibility for his neighbor's religion—he is his neighbor's priest or minister. The Reformation gave the volunteer worker a brand new place in the Christian Church.

The Sunday school movement, dating from 1780, was a lay movement from the start. It opened far more avenues for service than laymen had before. Decade after decade the Church and the Sunday school existed side by side, and it looked as though never the twain would meet. But meet they did. The Sunday school has gradually become the church school. The minister has been given more and more responsibility for it. Furthermore, many local churches are finding it advisable to employ full-time, professionally trained leaders, such as directors of Christian education.

Nevertheless, protestantism depends for its very life on lay leadership. This is due partly to the Protestant view of the responsibility of each person for spiritual life and growth. It is due also to the very practical reason that we have no other way of getting the work of the church done. The average church of today has far more volunteer workers than paid workers. The statistics of one denomination show about thirty church school teachers and officers to every pastor. Add the other volunteer workers who give leadership in church groups, and there is a vast weight on the volunteer side of the balance.

The case for the volunteer worker does not rest merely on numbers. Christian nurture has progressed through volunteer service as it would never have progressed through professional service alone. Think of the effect on the volunteer workers themselves. Thousands of them have grown through accepting responsibility as they could never have grown through mere membership. Think of the effect which volunteer workers have had on others. Almost every one of us can testify that his own life was enriched by a teacher or group leader who took an interest in him.

The effect of the volunteer has not always been good, however. He sometimes lacks Christian commitment and training, and therefore his work is not as good as it ought to be. He can give only a small part of his time to church work. Therefore, he may not be able to do everything that goes with the assignment he has accepted.

However, because of the strength which laymen bring to the church, and because of the help they need in order to use that strength to best advantage, every church must be concerned about enlisting and developing volunteer workers.

The Nature of Leadership

Before we consider ways in which a church may develop volunteer leadership for its work, we need to consider leadership itself. What is it? What kind of leader does the church need? Our thinking about leadership has undergone gradual change, and it is well for us to see where that change is taking us.

The church of today is looking for *group-centered leaders*. The day of the prima-donna leader is past.

The need of today is for the leader who will help a group achieve purposes that the group accepts as important. The worth of the leader is judged by what happens in the group, not by what the leader does. The nature of this kind of leadership is that it is shared. Leadership is not the prerogative of the one who happens to be out in front, to be guarded jealously by him as his right. It is to be shared with anyone who can help the group achieve its goals.

Group-centered leadership is not easy. It calls for persons who are secure, sincere, and deeply interested in people. The person who is insecure, fearful of his position, jealous of rivals, cannot be a group-centered leader. Let us illustrate. A rural church needed more space, and its people undertook to build an addition to the church. While they discussed the need for space, the pastor was their leader. A farmer who knew a good deal about building was the leader when they planned to do much of the work themselves, because they could not afford to hire labor. During the building operation itself, a contractor was the one to whom they looked for guidance. When teachers realized that their work in the new quarters would be different from the old program, they found a nearby children's worker to help them find new directions. The project succeeded because each of these leaders, in turn, was perfectly willing to share the leadership role when another was in a better position than he to meet the current need of the church.

At least two other types of leader can be identified. One is the *autocratic leader,* the dictator. He assumes that he knows what is best for the group. He is successful as a leader if the members of the group accept his program. People may feel secure under his leadership but they do not grow. The purposes, the decisions, and the growth are his.

Another type is the *laissez-faire leader.* He knows that it is not good for the group to have him play the dictator. He goes to the other extreme. He exercises no control, allowing the group to drift where it will, in whatever direction the whim of the moment may suggest. Progress of the group is uncertain and spotty. People feel insecure. They want a change, even though it may bring them the leadership of a dictator.

Between the two is the group-centered, or democratic, leader. People grow as they work with him. The group makes progress, though sometimes slowly. In the long run, this type of leadership is best for the work of the church.

Basic Principles of Leadership Education

How to develop workers who will exercise this kind of leadership is one of our most difficult problems. The success of our efforts at Christian nurture depends on our ability to solve it. How can we help the church administrator find a solution that will work in his church?

To deal with the problem fully would require a whole book on this subject alone. We must, therefore, limit ourselves to setting forth some basic principles of leadership education.

It is difficult to decide what to list as a principle of leadership education and what not to list. Every principle of Christian education applies also to leadership education. What we say about learning any Christian truth applies to learning the understandings and the skills of leadership. We shall not try to say everything! Rather, we shall try to sort out the principles that deal specifically with the development of leadership, assuming that the church will follow the principles of good Christian education also.

Build the kind of church program that will lay a foundation for Christian service

The best leader is one who is already a committed Christian, who knows the church and its work, and who believes that the world needs the church. This kind of attitude does not grow up overnight, or during a six-weeks course. It grows out of years of Christian experience in home and church. He who has it can be helped to do significant work in a church. He who does not have it is not yet ready for leadership responsibility. Let the church, therefore, lay solid foundations for leadership by developing in all of its members a sense of mission, vocation, and commitment to Christ.

Assign responsibility

A church may succeed in a difficult task like that of developing leadership only if definite responsibility is assigned for it. This assignment should go to the same body that is responsible for over-all educational policy and program. This will usually be the board, commission, or committee on Christian education. It is well to appoint a committee on personnel which can work on leadership concerns between meetings and report periodically to the group as a whole. In the small church, this will be a small committee. It may be only the pastor and the church school superintendent. It is important, however, that the committee be responsible to an overhead body rather than that it should work purely on its own authority.

Provide motivation as well as knowledge and skill

It is not enough to expose a worker to new ideas and new ways in church work. He must somehow feel that these ideas and ways are important. He must want to understand them and use them. A leadership education program, therefore, must include inspiration, prayer, worship, Bible study, and a sense of the guidance of the Holy Spirit. The leader of such a program may not be content with objective presentation of knowledge and procedures. Let him believe in what he is doing with such contagion that people are moved to use what they learn through him.

Equip each person to do the particular job the church has asked him to do

Industrial training programs have served as good examples to church leaders at this point. The industrial trainer analyzes a job to be done into the steps required to do it. He finds trouble spots and works out clues to success. Then he works with the trainees as a group and individually until each is able to do the particular job for which he has been hired.

Church work is not as simple as most of the jobs for which industry trains workers. The objectives of the church are different from the objectives of industry. There are more variables in church work, for we are concerned with the motives and behavior of people, and people are forever changing. It is possible, however, to break down any church task into certain steps. And it is possible to find trouble spots and clues to success. We need to go much further than most of us have gone in the direction of equipping each person to do the particular job the church has assigned to him.

It will be good for a church to work out specific descriptions for each position filled by a volunteer worker. Let these descriptions come from the workers themselves rather than be imposed by the pastor or by the official body of the church. The descriptions should, however, be reviewed by the official body and suggestions for correlation and improvement made by it. The preparation of such job descriptions is not easy. It may be more of a chore than workers will care to assume. If this is the case, secure a prepared job description from your denomination or from the National Council of Churches. Then let workers revise that statement to make it fit them and their church.

Include both content and method

Content and method belong together. It is of doubtful value to help a teacher gain new understandings of the Bible unless the teacher also knows how to help his class gain such new understandings. Ways of teaching are of doubtful value unless they are used to teach a content that is sound from a Christian point of view. But is it not possible to teach content in one leadership education program and method in another? Theoretically it is possible, but practically it does not work too well. A good deal of time may elapse between one program and another. A given worker may attend one program and miss the other entirely. Let the church therefore relate content and method.

Provide experience in good patterns of church work

Each of us follows the pathways that are familiar. We do things the way we have done them or have seen them done. This is true, even though we have been told to do them differently. As someone put it, "We teach as we were taught, not as we were taught to teach." The leadership education program, therefore, should include more than reading and talking about new and better ways of doing the work of the church. It should include actual experience.

The best way of providing this experience is through work with an expert. Let the church assign the teacher-in-training to work as an apprentice with a good, experienced teacher. Or let the church send selected workers to laboratory schools where they observe the expert teacher at work and later do practice teaching under his guidance. Observation is another good way, but not so good as guided practice.

He who watches the expert at work learns much, especially if there is opportunity to talk with the expert afterwards. Films and filmstrips bring a far-off expert into any church. While they are not so helpful as the expert would be if he could be present in the flesh, they bring good teaching to us in a very real fashion. One advantage is that they can be shown over and over again, and the learner may discover something new each time. Whenever possible, bring actual experience into the training program.

Let the leadership education program itself be a good illustration of group work

Perhaps this is a corollary of the preceding principle, but we believe it deserves separate mention. The concept of leadership that was expressed early in this chapter places great emphasis on the experience of the group. The leader succeeds only if the group succeeds. This is as true of the leadership class as of any other church group. If this class is dominated by the leader, we can only expect that its members will dominate the groups they lead in the church. If the members of this class are responsibly involved, it is likely that they will encourage the same kind of responsible participation in their own church work.

The church that would have the type of leader described here must be able to do two things: find and enlist for service the best workers it has available: and help these workers to develop the commitment, the attitudes, and the skills required in church leadership.

Enlisting Church Workers

Enlisting church workers calls for more than an interview in which someone uses the techniques of salesmanship to get the prospective worker to say "yes." It is necessary to start a good deal further back.

Personnel policy needs to be established, in order that the worker may know the conditions in which he will work, in order that the person doing the interviewing may know what he is asking another to do, and in order that the church may be sure that the worker, once he accepts, will find church service a privilege rather than an unwelcome chore. This personnel policy should cover such items as the following: description of the different positions to be filled by volunteers in the church, tenure of office for each position, a rotation system, assistantships to provide for substitutes as needed and to provide leaders-in-training for the future, a record of potential workers with the interests and abilities of each.

A *personnel committee* should oversee the whole business of enlisting and developing church workers. This committee is selected by the official board or by the board of Christian education. Its purpose is to gather information about potential workers, to help enlist workers for emerging needs in the church, and to clear the requests and needs of different church organizations so needs may be met without friction. It is obvious that the larger the church the greater the need for such a committee. Even the small church, however, needs to have someone acting as a personnel committee.

Advance planning to meet personnel needs is necessary. Unhappy is the church that is constantly "scraping the bottom of the barrel" in its efforts to fill vacant positions. It is not easy to avoid this unhappy position, but advance planning will help a great deal. The church program year usually begins in the fall. That is the time teachers and group leaders are needed in largest numbers. The next greatest need comes a few months later with the beginning of the new calendar year. Let the personnel committee face these needs, not in September or December but in April and May!

Let each organized group in the church indicate in April its probable leadership needs for the following fall and winter. Most of these needs can be anticipated. Any organization can know in advance when terms of office will close, what persons are likely to go away to school or to work, what persons should be relieved of responsibility because of family situations or the pressure of other duties. The church that anticipates its leadership needs can look at all of them together. It can challenge the right person for each job much better than can the church that tries to meet each need as it appears. The individual worker is benefited also. With advance notice of his selection to teach a class or lead a group, a person can observe, read, take training courses, and otherwise fit himself to render acceptable service. Advance planning is the key to many of the church's leadership difficulties.

Where can a church find people to fill its volunteer positions? The best answer is to establish a personnel file. Such a file lists the leaders and potential leaders of the church. It shows their background and training, their previous experience, and the interests and abilities that each is willing to use in the service of the church. This calls for a card file, with a card for each person. It is the task of the personnel committee to establish this file and keep it up to date. Let not the minister or church school superintendent say, "We know our people. We don't need a personnel file." Even the pastor of a small church cannot know and remember all the facts about background and interest of his people, especially the new ones as they move into the community.

The church that has not established its personnel file should lose no time in doing so. Some such device as the *Volunteer Christian Service* card will help. It may be circulated at the time of the every-member canvass, or when a new pastor begins service in a church, or with individual families as they move into the community. Cards or check lists for use in registration may be purchased in quantity from the National Council of Churches or from the denominational boards of Christian education. A church may prefer to print or mimeograph its own form. It should give people an opportunity to check their experience and interest in such types of service as are listed below.

- Ushering
- Leading Groups
  - Camping
  - Scouting
  - Youth Clubs
  - Hobby Groups
- Directing Music
- Organist
- Instrumental Music
- Vocal Music
- Evangelism
- Finance
- Interchurch Co-operation
- Missions
- Community Welfare
- Industrial Relations
- Intergroup Relations
- Home Visitation
- Baby Sitting
- Public Speaking
- Publicity
- Telephoning
- Correspondence
- Typing
- Mimeographing
- Nursing
- Cooking
- Decorations
- Art Work
- Crafts
- Photography
- Audio-Visuals
- Projectionist
- Radio-Television
- Dramatics
- Recreation
  - Athletics
  - Folk Games
  - Nature Lore
- Church School Superintendent
- Departmental Superintendent
  - Children
  - Youth
  - Adult
- Teacher
  - Children
  - Youth
  - Adult
  - Older Adults
- Nursery Roll
- Home Department
- Librarian
- Pianist
- Secretary
- Work with Families
- Vacation Church School Work
- Weekday Church School Work

From the information which it has assembled the personnel committee, in consultation with the various organizations of the church, selects the people to be invited to serve. Selections should be made in a spirit of prayer, of concern for the work of the groups involved, of concern for the growth of the persons and of concern for the relationships that will result. This is not a casual selection, as one chooses pieces for a jig-saw puzzle. This selection affects the Christian growth of persons. For someone it may be a matter of spiritual life or death. Let the choice be prayerfully and carefully made!

Only when these steps have been taken is the church ready for the *enlistment interview*. The same concerns which apply to selection apply to the interview in which the person selected is challenged to accept responsibility. In addition, there are some techniques which will be helpful. Give the invitation in person. Do not rely on announcements, on letters, or even on phone calls. Go in pairs. Let one person represent the church as a whole and the other person the department or organization to be served. If the person to be interviewed is likely to raise a particular kind of objection, let one of the interviewers be a person who has faced that same objection in his own church service. Be specific and frank about the responsibility involved. Show the person why he is "the man for the job." Show the help which the church is prepared to offer in order that the work may be done well. Help the person know the kind of group and program in which he will work, and the needs and opportunities which it affords. Show the place of the group and its program in the work of the church as a whole. Do not press too quickly for a final answer. Do not let the interview dangle, either. If the person accepts, express your appreciation and that of the church. If the person cannot accept at once, arrange for time when the final answer can be given. Be sure that the new worker knows what the next steps are in his preparation and in his beginnings in service. Let the interview be based on the commitment to Christ and his Church which is involved in church membership and which calls on each to give something of himself in the work of the church.

Elements in the Local Church Plan for Developing Workers

The church has by no means fulfilled its responsibility when it has assigned workers to each leadership position in the church. For these persons and for other workers-in-training there is need for a plan for developing in workers the commitments, the attitudes, and the skills which they will need in church service. Every church, either alone or in co-operation with other churches, should provide these elements.

The Workers' Conference which brings workers together for inspiration, for training, for planning, and for sharing of ideas. This is not a business meeting.

Reading of books and periodicals which relate to the church, to the particular age group, and to special curriculum units or program emphases.

Coaching and supervision through which the church provides experienced people to help workers fulfill their responsibilities.

Apprenticeship in which a beginner works with a veteran and learns in the process. Care must be taken to choose a veteran who is skilled, consecrated, and patient.

Observation through which one church worker learns by watching another. Care must be taken to select the worker to be observed so that the observer will see a good program in action.

The Leadership Class in which a group of people study some phase of church work that they may be able to serve more effectively. The denominations, working together through the National Council of Churches, have developed the Standard Leadership Curriculum for use in these classes. This curriculum is much the same wherever it is used. Most churches should have continuous training classes in their own program. They should also encourage their workers to enroll in training schools sponsored by the denomination, by the council of churches, or ministerial association. Some denominations, in addition, have prepared certain courses and textbooks of their own. When planning for a training class it is well to check with your denomination or council of churches to be sure that you have the latest bulletin or handbook, for these materials are frequently revised.

Personnel and program of the denomination and the council of churches, which exist primarily to serve the local church. The church should know what services are available, and should make good use of them. Among the most helpful services provided by staff persons are visits to individual churches to observe the work of the church and to counsel with church leaders. Among the most helpful programs offered by denominational and interdenominational agencies are laboratory schools and special institutes and conferences.

No church is so small that it cannot use each of these seven program elements to advantage. In some instances, the church will do these things in co-operation with others. Nearby churches which use the same curriculum materials may well hold quarterly workers' conferences together. A community library may well serve the reading needs of several churches. The leadership class or school is often sponsored by a group of co-operating churches. The responsibility for making the best use of these program elements, however, rests on the local church.

CHAPTER VII

Pupils and Program

Grouping and Grading

Most churches have far too many people to warrant keeping them together in one group for all of their church experiences. Furthermore, people of different ages vary considerably in their interests, abilities, and needs. Here, in two short sentences, are the reasons churches divide people into groups and have had to establish a policy with respect to grading.

Principles of Grouping and Grading

Experience has shown that churches are guided by three basic principles in determining the groups that shall be established.

Groups should consist of people of similar experience and ability who can and will work together. For children, the public school grade is usually the best basis for church grading. A child's playmates and friends are likely to be in his school grade. He is with them much of the week. It is natural, therefore, that he be with them in the church.

Any group should be large enough to permit a varied program, and small enough to encourage each individual to be an active member of it. Just how many persons this means for a given church school group or department is hard to say. The present trend is toward larger numbers of children in one room—divided into interest groups. This means that in addition to a leading teacher in each room, there should be helping teachers in the ratios indicated below:

A maximum of 8 or 10 two-year-olds in one room with a leader for every 4 to 6 children. (At least 2 adult leaders in any one room.)

A maximum of 15 three-year-olds in one room with a leader for every 4 to 6 children. (At least 2 adult leaders in any one room.)

A maximum of 20 kindergarten children in one room with a leader for every 5 to 8 pupils.

A maximum of 20 to 25 primary children in one room with a leader for every 8 to 10 pupils.

A maximum of 20 to 25 junior children in one room with a leader for every 8 to 10 pupils.

For youth and adults, groups of twenty to twenty-five are preferable. Each person can hold a responsible place in a group of this size. The trend is away from the large adult Bible classes of former years. In a class of seventy-five or one hundred there are too many silent partners.

The number of groups is often determined by such practical considerations as the number of capable leaders and the amount of space available.

The Traditional Departments

The divisions and departments that have been commonly accepted in the Sunday church school are these:

Children's Division	
Nursery Department	Under 4 years
Kindergarten Department	Ages 4, 5
Primary Department	Grades 1, 2, 3
Junior Department	Grades 4, 5, 6
Youth Division	
Junior High Department	Grades 7, 8, 9
Senior High Department	Grades 10, 11, 12
Post High Department	High school graduation to young adulthood
Adult Division	
Young Adults	Bases indicated below
Adults	Divided according to age or interest
Older Adults	

The basis for grading is clear in each department through the senior high. Difficulty does not arise often in grading children and youth.

There is no one basis for deciding when a person should enter or leave the young adult department. A person becomes a young adult gradually. It is usually agreed that a person should enter a young adult group when he has had three or four of the following "transition experiences": leaving school, achieving self-support, marriage, leaving the parental home, reaching voting age, discharge from military service. The question as to when a person leaves the young adult department is part of the special question about grouping adults which is considered below.

Adaptations Because of Size

Most churches do not have eight different departments, each with its separate meeting place. They lack either the numbers of people or the space or both. They find it necessary to make some kind of combination. Combinations range all the way from four classes in a one-room church to the separate department for each grade which the large church may require.

A chart suggesting various combinations of grouping is reproduced here from the *International Journal of Religious Education.*

Even the smallest church should have the four groups suggested in the first line of the chart. The larger church will find the desired combination of groups farther down in the chart. Large churches may have a separate group for *each year or school grade.*

<table>
<tr><th colspan="6">AGE GROUP</th><th colspan="4">GRADES</th><th colspan="8">AGE GROUP</th></tr>
<tr><td colspan="6">Pre-school</td><td colspan="2">1–6</td><td colspan="2">7–12</td><td colspan="8">Over 17</td></tr>
<tr><td colspan="6">Pre-school</td><td>1–3</td><td>4–6</td><td colspan="2">7–12</td><td colspan="8">Over 17</td></tr>
<tr><td colspan="6">Pre-school</td><td>1–3</td><td>4–6</td><td>7–9</td><td>10–12</td><td colspan="8">Over 17</td></tr>
<tr><td colspan="3">Under 4 years</td><td colspan="3">4–5 years</td><td>1–3</td><td>4–6</td><td>7–9</td><td>10–12</td><td colspan="4">Older Youth 18–23</td><td colspan="4">Over 24</td></tr>
<tr><td colspan="2">Under 3</td><td colspan="2">3</td><td colspan="2">4, 5 years</td><td>1–3</td><td>4–6</td><td>7–9</td><td>10–12</td><td colspan="2">Older Youth 18–23</td><td colspan="4">Young Adults 24–35</td><td colspan="2">Over 35</td></tr>
<tr><td>Under 2</td><td colspan="2">2</td><td colspan="2">3</td><td>4, 5</td><td>1, 2</td><td>3, 4</td><td>5, 6</td><td>7–9</td><td>10–12</td><td colspan="2">Older Youth 18–23</td><td colspan="2">Young Adults 24–35</td><td colspan="2">Adults 36–65</td><td>Older Adults over 65</td></tr>
</table>

Some Questions about Grouping and Grading

Four questions about grouping and grading come up so persistently that they deserve special comment here.

What about the church's program for children under three?

The church's ministry to children of this age is primarily through the home. It should center in help for parents which includes both guidance for the religious nurture of children and spiritual enrichment for themselves.

There is a very real question as to whether children should be brought together in groups at the church before the age of two or three because of the physical and emotional needs of the earliest years. However, if such group care is provided it is recommended that the church meet the following conditions:

> Mature Christian leadership, trained for work with the age involved. (Understanding differences in individual children is important among qualifications.)
>
> Plans made for ongoing training program to assure continuing supply of trained leadership.
>
> Consistent leadership personnel (at least one of the adults with each group to carry continuous responsibility from week to week).
>
> Close relationship of program to remainder of nursery work (probably under supervision of nursery superintendent).
>
> Adequate provision for sanitary facilities: washable warm floors, clean linens for every child for each use, in case of crib or play pens.
>
> Washable toys, selected from designated listing.
>
> Inspection by nurse or other trained person and exclusion of children with colds or other symptoms.
>
> For toddlers: one child-sized toilet to ten children; one washbowl to eight children.
>
> Easily available facilities for heating bottles.
>
> Space: for crib babies: three feet between cribs.
> for toddlers: minimum of thirty square feet per child.[1]
>
> A separate place for not more than twelve crib babies.
>
> A separate place for not more than eight toddlers (under two).[1]
>
> One adult to three or four babies; one adult to every four toddlers; never one adult alone.[1]
>
> Assurance of ready accessibility of parents.
>
> Conferences with parents and leaders in advance of admission, and periodically thereafter.
>
> Assurance that parent will stay with child until he feels secure (recognizing differences in individual children and at different age levels).
>
> Continuing consideration by planning group of ways in which parents may be helped by the church in the guidance of their

[1] For leadership and space needs for two-year-olds, see pp. 70 and 85.

children. (Parent groups, counsel by qualified staff person, home visits by trained workers, etc.)

Continuous evaluation and planning with parent participating.

Provision for leader to take child who may have become ill or upset away from others until parent can be secured.

Also desirable:

Adjoining space for conferences with parents, and for parents to wait when determining whether child is ready to be left.

Direct entrance from outside; first floor location.

Ample storage and supply space.

Low windows with clear glass.

What about separate classes for boys and girls?

There is no doubt that there are psychological differences between boys and girls, and that these differences have a bearing on church work with them. These differences are especially noticeable in the junior and junior high departments. Girls are definitely more mature than boys during this period, and their interests and abilities differ accordingly. This fact has led some to conclude that boys and girls should be separated, at least in these two departments.

Before a church reaches such a conclusion, however, it should note two facts. One is that life (including school) is co-educational. It is logical to have boys and girls face the truths of religion together just as they face other phases of life together. The other fact is that differences from one age to another are just as real as differences between the sexes. This creates a problem for the small church if it tries to create separate classes for boys and girls. There is more psychological difference, for example, between a second grade boy and a sixth grade boy than there is between a sixth grade boy and a sixth grade girl.

What about grouping adults?

Logically, we should establish graded classes for adults as we do for children and we should promote people from one group to another when they reach a given point in age or experience. Practically, however, this is difficult to do. There are no neat dividing lines for adults. And besides, many adults resent a grouping which is imposed on them.

Adult grouping usually becomes a problem in the church when young adults feel that existing adult groups are "too old" for them. The most practical solution is to start a new young adult group when this happens. The existing adult groups continue. Now and then it becomes possible to combine two or more of the older classes. This seems like a haphazard method, but it works fairly well.

Another solution is to divide adult groups according to interest rather than age. This method should be more widely used as there is much to commend it. Let the church school set up an elective curriculum for adults, with choices that are varied enough to appeal to different interests and numerous enough to make classes of manageable size. These groups remain together only until the courses are completed, and then a new election of courses creates new groups. The social needs of people may be met through some type of continuing organization, perhaps the usual men's and women's organizations of the church.

What about the two-grade department?

Children's workers remind us that there is considerable difference between the first-grader and the third-grader. It is very difficult for the primary department worker to challenge the one and be understood by the other at the same time. The same difference exists in the junior department between the fourth and sixth grades. There is no problem for the church that is large enough to have a separate department for each school grade. But what about average and small churches?

There is a definite trend toward two-grade departments as the answer to this problem. It provides a primary department consisting of grades 1 and 2. A lower junior department is added for grades 3 and 4. Grades 5 and 6 make up the upper junior department. Denominations which provide separate curriculum materials for the lower junior department report large demand for it. New educational buildings are increasingly providing for two-grade departments in the children's division, and in some cases in junior high and senior high departments.

Promotion

A system of grouping requires some plan by which pupils advance from one class or department to another. The term, "promotion," is commonly used for this advancement. It is important that promotion be handled in such a manner that it has meaning for the child. Church school publications contain many suggestions as to how this may be done.

A question that the administrator faces is that of the best time for promotion. Some say that June is the best time, since that is when pupils advance from one school grade to another. Any promotion that comes later is an anti-climax. Others say that fall is the best time, probably a Sunday in September. The church school year usually begins then, and curriculum units change. Therefore this is a good time for promotion. Furthermore, fall promotion makes grading in the vacation church school or summer conference easier. If promotion comes in June, it is difficult to put a vacation church school pupil in the grade from which the Sunday church school has just promoted him. To advance him to the new grade, however, often means that vacation church school material is too difficult for him. Let the administrator take these factors into account, consult his own denomination for recommendations, and then decide what promotion time is best for his church school.

Records and Reports

Records aid the church in Christian nurture in two ways. They preserve information for the future—information about the church and its program and also about people. They bring together facts about the church and its work in such a way that church leaders may study these facts and find ways to improve the church's program.

Six types of records deserve to be preserved, each in its own way.

The separate record of each organization

This is important for future planning by the organization. Our memories are not sufficient. The organizational record should include such items as these: minutes of business meetings, record of membership and attendance, list of officers and committees, record of projects and activities, and copies of printed or mimeographed materials.

Cumulative pupil's record

In addition to personal data (address, telephone number, birthday, etc.), this record shows date of enrollment in the church school, curriculum units the pupil has used, special interests and abilities, and special service rendered.

Cumulative leader's record

This record shows the church work the person has done, special interests or abilities he has, and training which he has had. Potential leaders should be included, as well as those now in service. This record, therefore, is a valuable aid in discovering new leadership. It should be kept up to date by addition of new items of information.

Responsibility list

On this list should go the names of unreached people. A list should be kept for the church as a whole, and also for individual groups and organizations. This is part of the church's plan of evangelism.

Financial record

Important financial records include the treasurer's record of income and expenditures. They also include the budget for the current year, with information to show how well the organization is living within its budget.

Confidential record for the group leader himself

Every teacher finds it important to know his pupils individually. Gradually he acquires information which is not common knowledge. He discovers attitudes, habits, strengths, and weaknesses. It is difficult to remember all these personal insights. It is especially difficult to recall the partial insights that come, piece by piece, as he is learning to know a given pupil. Many teachers have found it helpful to keep a confidential notebook in which pertinent bits of information are recorded from time to time. This notebook preserves what the memory often loses. It keeps odd bits of information which later fit together and give the teacher valuable guidance. This notebook must not be common property. It is confidential to the teacher, and is usually not even given to the person who teaches the class next year.

Records become the basis for reports through which an organization gives information about itself and its work. Educational groups in the church should plan for at least three kinds of report.

Regular reports should be made to the board of Christian education, since educational groups are responsible to it. The board should know how the organization is getting along. This means, of course, facts about enrollment, attendance, and needs. It also means reports on the spirit of the group and the extent to which it is accomplishing the purposes which the church expects of it. Difficulties or questions should be reported to the board for counsel and help.

Occasional reports should go to the congregation as a whole. Usually there is an annual report which is designed to cover the entire work of the church. The form of this report is determined by the congregation itself. Written reports, submitted in advance and duplicated, are far better than reports which must be read in an annual meeting. Let the reports in the annual meeting be brief, varied, and full of flavor. The written report should cover the facts. Organizations often report to the congregation informally through items in newsletters or church bulletins.

A third type of report which is difficult yet important is a report to parents. They ought to know what has been accomplished and what is being planned in the church groups to which their children belong. This kind of reporting is best done through letters and special parents' meetings. Parents ought also to know how well their children are participating in the group program. This calls for some type of individual progress report. A "report card" with grades assigned to each pupil is hardly desirable. Rather, we suggest a report form which shows regularity and punctuality of attendance and which also reflects the quality of participation. A state educational committee[1] suggests a progress report on which the teacher checks each pupil's participation under the headings "usually," "frequently," or "seldom" on each of eight items. The eight items are "gets the facts . . . appreciates the meaning of the facts . . . learns the memory work . . . passes the tests . . . participates in class discussion . . . shares in group activities . . . gets along with other pupils . . . shows reverence in worship."

The church which wishes to use such a report to parents should develop its own form, giving parents and children an opportunity to help determine its content. With this kind of participation the resulting form is likely to fit into the program of the particular church. It is also likely to arouse less resistance and misunderstanding than would a report form taken from some outside source.

Cultivating Attendance

The church which takes its work seriously must be concerned about reaching people. It wants regular attendance. It wants a high average of attendance. But the concern is more than statistical. It is essential that every person be involved in Christian nurture. The church cannot be content until it has reached every man, woman, and child in the area which that church serves. Every person is a child of God, regardless of social standing, economic status, race, or color. Every one of these persons, therefore, is part of the evangelistic concern of the church. This concern should result in unceasing efforts to reach those who are now unreached and untaught and in efforts to secure regular attendance by those who are reached.

The unreached must be found before they can be reached. The most thorough way of finding them is the religious census, which is a door-to-door visitation to discover the religious membership or preference of every person in the community. If the census is complete, it puts every person in the community either on the membership list or on the responsibility list of some church. The census is best when it is made by the churches in co-operation. It then shows the concern of all the churches, and does not appear as the effort of one par-

[1] The Committee on Religious Education of the Massachusetts Congregational Conference.

ticular church to get ahead. Guidance for the census and materials for use in it are available from most denominations and from the National Council of Churches.

Another way to find some of the unreached is to check new arrivals through lists compiled by public utilities companies or through the "Welcome Wagon."

A particular church organization may profit by checking the membership rolls of other groups. Every member of the church, for example, is a potential member of the appropriate church school class. The roll of the vacation church school and the weekday church school may include persons who should be in the Sunday church school. Also, a check of former membership lists may show persons who dropped out at one time but may be reached now.

Whatever the means by which a responsibility list may be compiled, the next step is visitation. Someone visits the unreached person, tells him of the program of the church, and invites him to become a part of it. The visitor makes a report so that the church may know what progress is being made. It sometimes happens that one person is unable to make progress, but another may. In such cases, the prospective member should be assigned to another visitor. The purpose of the visits is to help people, not to achieve a larger number on the roll. Visitors should be helped to realize the purpose and importance of their visits.

It is every bit as important to maintain regular attendance of members as it is to reach unreached persons. Little is gained by bringing people in at the front door of the church if they promptly slip out the back door because of indifference.

The two best ways to secure regular attendance are to build a good program and to draw people into active participation in it. People want to be in the group that meets their needs, and they will be regular in attendance. One way to be sure a program will meet the needs of a particular person is to draw him into responsible participation in it. If he helps to plan and conduct the program, his interests and needs will probably find expression in it. Program and participation are the two best clues to attendance.

Prompt and personal follow-up of absentees will help, too. Let a person know that he has been missed and he will feel closer to the group than if his absence is allowed to go unnoticed. A personal note is better than a form follow-up card. A telephone call is better than a note. A personal visit is best of all.

An important function of follow-up of absentees is to find the cause of the absence. If the cause is related to the program of the group, by all means find the way to attack that cause. The whole purpose back of our concern for regular attendance is not statistical but personal. People need Christian nurture, but they are not likely to get it if they are continually absent. Therefore cultivate attendance.

What about awards and contests? Much has been said, both pro and con, about them. Awards and contests often produce temporary increases in enrollment and attendance. The new members will remain, however, only if they find a program that is good and that meets their needs. It all goes back to basic purpose and motivation. The church that wants to extend real Christian nurture to more and more people needs more than awards and contests.

Everyone agrees that there is value in appropriate recognition of work well done. Awards systems that are based on attendance, however, have been questioned on such grounds as these:

> They are expensive. The money might better be spent in program improvement.
>
> They emphasize the wrong motivation. The pin is made to seem more important than the Christian growth which is the real purpose of the church school. Quantity (attendance) is made to seem more important than quality (participation).
>
> They may cause a health hazard if people insist on attending when they ought to stay at home. They endanger their own health and the health of others.
>
> The system of awards for attendance is a sign of defeat, for it indicates that the pupil is drawn not by the work of the church but by the award he hopes to receive. Quality of program is, in the long run, a better incentive to regular attendance than any system of awards.

Contests are of doubtful value, too. They tend to draw attention away from the main business of the church to the details of the contest. They tend to divide the church into competing groups, and sometimes the heat of competion causes ill will that outlasts the contest. If the energy required to win the contest were put into creative Christian effort, the resulting program probably would draw larger attendance and hold it longer than the contest.

CHAPTER VIII

Building and Equipment

The Building Also Teaches

Each of the factors mentioned in earlier pages makes a difference in Christian nurture. Organization, administration, program building, leadership—these are of primary importance. If the history of Christian nurture were completely told, there would be many chapters about leaders who brought about remarkable growth in persons in spite of poor equipment. There would be others where leaders without consecration and imagination did poorly in spite of good equipment. It is still true, however, that good physical environment helps and poor environment hinders the process of Christian nurture.

The building sets limits on program. Any building contains a given number of rooms. The number and location of these rooms determines the number of groups that can meet in the church. The size of these rooms limits the number of persons whom the church can serve. There is, for example, the congregation in a growing community that built a new sanctuary beside its original building. Their intention was to remodel the original building, using all of it for age-group programs. They were amazed and chagrined to discover that no amount of remodeling would make that building adequate, for there simply was not enough floor space in it. In spite of human ingenuity, the building does set limits.

Building and equipment that are adequate encourage good church work. In a room that has sufficient space for an activity program it is less likely that teachers will keep children sitting in tight rows. In a church that provides equipment for a varied teaching program it is not likely that teachers will simply "talk at" children. The very process of deciding what space and equipment are needed may open the eyes of teachers to their use. Good building and equipment *encourage* good work with church groups, but *they do not guarantee* good work.

Building and equipment have an effect on the spirit of young and old alike. A well equipped church suggests to its people that religion is important and that they are fortunate to be members of that church. This is a good feeling if, then, it leads people to want to work in that church and not merely to feel proud. A church whose building is poorly equipped, poorly maintained, and out-of-date suggests to its people that religion is unimportant. They are likely to feel that nothing they do in the church will make a real difference either for them or for the society of which they are part. Let the church, then, provide the best building and equipment it can, in order that people may be encouraged in their spiritual growth. The Appendix suggests sources to which the administrator may go for detailed guidance about building and equipment. Here we shall list some of the guiding principles which a church should keep in mind as it seeks to improve its building and equipment.

Some Guiding Principles in Preparing to Build

Study the needs of the church and its people

How many people are there in each age group? The chart on grading which appears in Chapter 7 will help determine the number of groups for which to plan. Take into account the trends in population growth. The increased birth rate of the forties and fifties will mean an increase in different age groups as the wave of increase reaches them. Moreover, there are local variations which need to be taken into account. It makes a difference whether a congregation of two hundred members is building in a growing community with young families, or in a static community with few young families.

Investigate the needs of each age group. What is being provided for them now, by the church and by other agencies in the community? What more do they need if they are to grow as Christians?

Think through the program required

Keep in mind the location of other church buildings in which Christian programs will also be provided. Keep in mind the nearness of community facilities for fellowship and group work. Keep in mind the various organized groups that will be using church facilities—church school, scouts, youth center, young adults, older adults, service groups of various kinds, community groups that look to the church for support. A complete statement showing the program, membership, and needs of the church and its related organizations should be prepared before a line is drawn on blueprint paper. This planning should be done, not by a small building committee alone, but by as representative a committee, or group of committees, as can be enlisted.

Enlist all organizations in the planning process

Invite each organization to consider carefully its own needs and program and then submit its requests. When these various requests have been put together, the result will be both a better plan and better support for the building project. This kind of planning takes time, but Christian nurture is important enough to deserve time in planning the building and facilities for it.

See what other churches have done

A tremendous amount of church school building has been done in recent years. No church can afford to embark on a building venture of its own without profiting by the experience of these other churches. This can best be done by visiting church school buildings that have recently been completed. If possible, include several churches with about the same number of members and about the same conditions as the church that plans to build. In addition to visiting, it is well to get information by reading about other building projects and by consultation with people who have had experience in building for Christian nurture. Valuable help can be secured from denominational departments of architecture and from the Bureau of Church Building of the National Council of Churches.

Determine the rooms and equipment needed

The requests of various organizations and the suggestions that come from many sources must be put together into one set of specifications for the building. This might be done by the board of Christian education or by a subcommittee appointed by the board. These specifications should include the number of rooms needed, the number of persons to be served in each, and suggested floor space. Remember that administrators also need space for a desk or office. Specifications should also include detailed suggestions regarding equipment and facilities needed for the program. The building committee then works out, with architect, consultants, and builders, the best ways to provide these facilities.

Keep the congregation informed and unified

A united church can almost always work out a suitable answer to its building problems. A divided church is in trouble. Therefore, keep the congregation informed about the need for additional facilities and about progress toward meeting that need. Take into account suggestions, objections and questions. There comes a time, of course, when the welfare of the church demands action and it would be unwise to allow further delay to win over a small minority. The more nearly unanimous the agreement, however, the easier it is to complete the building project. Let the work of building a church become an educational—and religious—experience for the entire congregation.

Develop leadership

The new facilities will provide new opportunities for church program. These advances, however, will not come by themselves. Do not wait until the building is completed and hope that new program will emerge. Rather, make plans to develop leadership at the time the physical plant is being built. Only so can a new day be assured for the church.

Some Guiding Principles for the Building Itself

House the entire church program in one building, or in connecting units

The church has one basic purpose in all phases of its program, namely: to develop Christian persons and a Christian society. Let the church building, therefore, be a symbol of this unity of purpose.

There is practical as well as symbolic reasoning in favor of having unity in the church building. The movement of people from room to room and from group to group is made easy if the building is a unit. Heating and janitorial services are simplified. Maintenance problems in general are met more easily in one building than in separate buildings.

Provide large areas of floor space which may be divided by nonsupporting partitions

There are at least two factors which favor this principle. One is the present trend away from the "cubby-hole" classroom (where activities are likely to be limited to lecture or discussion) and toward the larger working space which is required for a varied program. The suggestions of floor space which are given below reflect this trend.

The other factor is flexibility. The small classroom can be used solely for a very few people. The larger area may be used by various groups in various ways, according to changing numbers and programs. The current trend is definitely toward separate rooms for the different age groups. (See floor space and pupil enrollment suggestions below.)

Flexibility is further assured by separating rooms with walls that are not load-bearing. These may be moved, if necessary, without affecting the building itself. In general, such walls are better than sliding doors or folding partitions. Movable partitions are not soundproof. They are expensive to install and may cause maintenance problems. There are, of course, conditions under which the movable partition is the best answer, but other solutions should be explored first.

Provide adequate floor space for each group

There is no rule of thumb by which a church may know just how much space to allocate to a given group. A general rule is: The younger the pupil the more space is needed. The chart below is based on wide experience and will provide general guidance. A good procedure is to measure off the suggested floor space in a larger room, and then try out the kind of program that is desired, using the equipment and the number of children for which a church needs to plan. This kind of trial will show whether the suggested floor space per person is adequate for your group. It may also help to convince members of a building committee that generous space allocation is needed for younger groups.

Floor Space Suggestions

Age Group	*Maximum Pupils per Room*	*Floor Space per Pupil*
Nursery		
Two-year olds[1]	8-10	30-35 sq. ft.
Three-year-olds	15	25-35 sq. ft.
Kindergarten	20	25-35 sq. ft.
Primary	20-25	25-30 sq. ft.
Junior	20-25	25-30 sq. ft.
Junior High	20	15-18 sq. ft.
Senior High	25	15-18 sq. ft.
Post High	25	15-18 sq. ft.
Adult	25	10 sq. ft.

The figures given under "Maximum Pupils per Room" do not suggest that this number of persons should be in one class or teaching group, with one leader in charge of each. Part of the time the group will divide into smaller working units or interest groups. When this happens there will be need for a number of leaders, as has been suggested earlier. When enrollment in a children's group is above the number indicated, attention should be given to the two-grade or the single-grade grouping. When the single-grade grouping is used one room should be large enough to allow the whole department to meet together.

---

[1] When care is provided for children under age three, see Chapter 7 for guidance regarding this matter.

Include in each room provision for all the activities that enter into a complete program

The program will include worship, study, discussion, recreation, dramatization, music, and use of audio-visual materials. Each of these has a place in learning. The use of each will vary somewhat from age group to age group. An adequate building permits free use of all of them in their varied forms.

For worship neither chapels nor permanent worship centers are recommended for church school use. For youth and adults emphasis should be on the congregational worship opportunities in the church. For children worship is best that is closely related to their other activities of work and study in their own rooms.

Arrange for each room to open off a corridor leading to the main building

Such arrangement permits use of the room by different age groups, if changes in enrollment or program should suggest reassignment of rooms. There is also less danger in case of fire or other emergency.

Locate certain departments on the ground floor

This is especially important for nursery and kindergarten children. These two groups should also be located near an outside exit to make convenient the use of out-of-doors for activity. Young children are often disturbed by a long walk through a crowded corridor. Easy access is an aid to parents as they bring to the church school and meet them at the close of the session. It is also an added safety precaution in case of fire.

It is desirable that rooms where their parents meet be easily accessible to rooms used by nursery and kindergarten children. Rooms to be used by older adults should be so located as to avoid flights of stairs.

Lavatories should be convenient

Except for small buildings, lavatories should be located on each floor. For small children, lavatories should be in or near the room, and should be equipped with child-size fixtures.

Usually rooms should be rectangular, with one unbroken wall

Generally the rectangular room (ratio of about four to five) lends itself best to various arrangements of furniture and equipment. One wall should be unbroken by windows, doors, chalk boards, cabinets, or offsets. This is the wall which the group will face in group sessions. This also affords a suitable place to arrange an interest center.

Windows should provide a maximum of light, without glare

Glass should be clear, especially for children's groups. There may be an appropriate medallion, but otherwise the glass should be clear. The windows should be low enough to permit children to see out while standing on the floor. The window construction should, however, be of such type as to keep children from falling out. To assure adequate light, window area should conform to the state building codes.

Ventilation should be considered

Ventilation should be provided which is independent of transoms and doorways, for there are times when these must be closed. Likewise, ventilation should be so planned that it will not be cut off when shades are used to darken windows during film projection.

Provide storage space in each room as well as general storage

Storage space in each room should provide open shelves scaled to the age group, storage cabinets for teaching supplies, pictures, paper, and other materials.

Provide clothing racks

They should be high enough to accommodate clothing of the age group for whom the room is intended, yet low enough that children can take care of their own clothes. Let there also be provision for the teacher's wraps. Clothes racks should be near the entrance to the room.

Some Guiding Principles Regarding Equipment

Floor covering should be durable, warm, and easily cleaned

Hardwood, asphalt tile, rubber tile, and inlaid linoleum are the most generally accepted materials for flooring. Washable rugs are a welcome addition for nursery and kindergarten, because children spend a good deal of time on the floor. Be sure, however, that the rugs are washed! Floors should never be oiled in children's departments. Care should be taken that the floors are not slippery.

Color is important

Plenty of color may be used in room decoration but experienced counsel should be sought in choosing color. The architect is generally the best person to suggest color schemes. Paint companies sometimes provide advisory service. The atmosphere of the room and its impression upon the pupil coming into the room is important in Christian education. Color should be determined by desired atmosphere of warmth, coolness, or exhilaration. Generally, heavy dark colors should be avoided.

Good artificial lighting is necessary

No amount of window space will provide enough light on a cloudy day. Then, of course, there are the late afternoon and evening sessions which may be held in any room. The type and location of light fixtures should be such as to avoid glare.

Darkening facilities are important

Adequate provision should be made for darkening the windows in each room so that projected audio-visuals may be used effectively during the daytime.

Select pictures carefully

Pictures are valued aids to teaching, and should be used as such. In addition to the unframed teaching pictures there may be well chosen framed pictures. They should not be changed each week, nor should they be allowed to remain indefinitely.

Provide chalk boards or turnover charts

These are essential for the primary and older groups. The teacher or leader should have some way of placing before the group such materials as a verse of Scripture, a stanza of a hymn, a prayer the group has composed, an idea for next week, or a decision the group has reached. For this reason the movable blackboard, or chalk board, has become standard equipment in the up-to-date church school. The turnover chart, consisting of a pad of paper on some sort of easel, is becoming increasingly popular. It is portable. It permits a leader to keep material over a period of many weeks, simply turning back to an earlier page when there is need to refer to material used in the past. Furthermore, the chart is free of the dust that the chalk board brings.

Chairs and tables should be of appropriate height

Chairs should be sturdy and durable, yet light in weight and preferably in natural finish. Folding chairs should be avoided for children's groups. It is always good to check the heights of chairs to be sure that the particular children will find them suitable. In general the following heights are standard: nursery—eight inches; kindergarten—ten inches; primary—fourteen inches; junior—sixteen inches. Tables should be approximately ten inches higher than chair seats.

Special Concerns in Remodeling

The principles mentioned in previous pages apply to remodeling just as much as they apply to new construction. There are, however, some considerations which apply especially to remodeling. We call attention to a few of these.

Develop a long-range plan

It often happens that a congregation decides on renovation because it cannot afford an entirely new building. Let that church plan the kind of building it wants for its people and program. Then let the committee undertake a remodeling project which will meet the most urgent needs at present and which will also move in the direction of the long-range plan. Such long-range planning is more satisfactory than to make a few changes here and a few there without looking ahead.

Visit similar remodeling projects

It is harder to do a satisfactory remodeling job than to build a new building. The reason, of course, is obvious. The committee is trying to meet all the needs of people and program but is limited by the old building. Some churches have shown amazing ingenuity in remodeling. It will be good for any church which considers remodeling to visit those who have done similar jobs in order to learn from them.

Anticipate changes in the flow of traffic

A few changes in a building often lead to surprising differences in the movement of people from room to room and from group to group. Let the committee ask itself such questions as these: What entrance will families use? How will parents go from nursery or kindergarten to the adult rooms? What entrance will older children and young people use? Where will the church school office be located? How will pastor, superintendents, and secretaries move from place to place? How will individual groups move to and from assembly rooms? How will individuals and groups move between church school and church services? What will be the relation of such special groups as the choir to church school rooms?

It is important to assign rooms so there may be a minimum amount of travel back and forth for parents and administrators. Groups and rooms should be so arranged that it is not necessary for anyone to pass through one room to get to another.

Space Shortage in the Church That Cannot Build

Thus far the discussion has assumed that the church can and will build or remodel as needed in order to serve its people more adequately. Time and again, however, a congregation confronts space shortage but is not able at that time to make major changes in its building. There are some steps that church can take to ease the situation temporarily. They are not as good as a building project, but they are far better than sitting idly by while the problem grows.

Change the church schedule by holding several sessions

As was suggested earlier, there are many ways in which this may be done. It is best for a given church to depend on local factors. Here are some possibilities:

Schedule two church school sessions, with the church worship service between. Each church school session may cover all ages, or one may include the younger departments and the other the older. In each instance, duplicate use of rooms allows the church to serve more people in the same space.

Schedule the older departments, beginning with the juniors, in one period and the younger departments during the church worship service. This schedule provides for some duplicate use of rooms. It is practicable only if the building has enough separate space to allow children's groups and those attending the worship service to meet at the same time without undue interference.

Hold two church school services and two worship services. In effect, this means dividing the church into two groups. Group A goes to church school first and to church worship second. Group B goes to church worship first and to church school second. Members choose their own preferred schedule rather than have an arbitrary division into groups.

None of these schedules is ideal. Each creates the need for more leaders than the traditional schedule. One of them would prevent church school workers in some departments from attending any church worship service. Each of them involves a close schedule on Sunday morning, with the need for a quick change of equipment and facilities when a room is used twice.

Use nearby space

It may be possible to buy or rent a house next to the church and to use that house for church school and parish house purposes. There may be a community building nearby in which space may be secured for Sunday use. Now and then space is available in the home of a member or friend. If the space is in a basement be sure that it is warm and dry. If the space is in living room or den be sure to assign to it groups that will not harm furnishings.

Provide portable facilities

Groups meeting in crowded churches are likely to have little in the way of equipment. Portable equipment may help to fill this need. A class meeting in the sanctuary, for example, has no facilities for writing. Lap boards, made of masonite or ply-wood, make excellent writing space and may be stored away easily at the close of the session. Children may even use the pews for writing or other paper work. If this is done, be sure to protect the pews from damage. Portable blackboards, or turnover charts on easels, may be a great help to the teacher who meets a class in the sanctuary.

Arrange separate areas for different age groups

This may be done even if the groups must meet in the same room. They may be separated by movable screens (not curtains). These screens can be removed completely and stored when not in use. When they are in use screens may be used as bulletin boards. They are not soundproof, of course, but they do keep groups from seeing each other.

If chairs are used they may be arranged in semi-circles for discussion purposes. It is easier for a group in a circle to work independently of others than for a group spread over straight rows to do so.

A small group of children may use its own private space. For example, a piano may be placed out from the wall, needed equipment set behind it, and the space used for activities suitable to the age group. The back of the piano may be covered and used as a display place for pictures or other materials.

Be sure that no suitable place has been overlooked. The kitchen may be better than a corner in an overcrowded room. A storage room may be cleaned out, painted, and used for a variety of purposes.

Whatever the decision, the church needs to remember that Christian nurture of people is its task. The building may hinder or the building may help. It is the function of the administrator to make the building contribute to the Christian growth of persons.

CHAPTER IX

Finance and Christian Nurture

The obvious purpose of church finance is to raise enough money to meet the costs of church program. Finance and program, however, are related in many ways that do not appear in the treasurer's records. The church teaches through the way it gets and spends money. The causes for which a church is willing to spend money show what that church considers important. People form their ideas of the worth of missions, of world service, of ministerial pensions, of benevolent institutions partly by the place the church budget gives to these causes. The church teaches through its own financial practice at least as much as it teaches through planned efforts at stewardship education.

The reverse is also true. The way in which a church teaches about the various causes represented in its budget affects the giving of its members to these causes. No clear line can be drawn between finance and nurture, for the two are inseparably related.

Principles Involved in Financing the Educational Program

The practices which churches follow in financing their educational programs differ widely. The practice of a particular church usually stems partly from the financial setup which it inherited from the past and partly from denominational policy. We believe it will be helpful to administrators if we identify some principles that are basic to good financial practice in any church. We deal here, of course, not with the whole financial program of the church but only with the points at which finance and Christian nurture are especially related.

Include the educational program in the total budget of the church

We assume that the church prepares a budget of income and expenditure and that it has a plan for underwriting that budget. Provision for Christian nurture should be made through that budget, and not through some supplementary financial plan. In this way the whole church recognizes its responsibility for Christian nurture. This is good. This also means that children and young people give not merely to the church school but to all the work of the church.

Use finance as an educational opportunity

Those who make up the budget should be educated in churchmanship. They should not merely prepare two sets of figures and see that they balance. They should study the program and opportunities of the church. They should weigh causes in order to determine what the church people shall be asked to support. Those who make the canvass should be educated, too. They must be informed about the church and its work. They must be prepared to answer questions and to give information about the various causes which are included in the budget. If they are good canvassers they must be enthusiastic supporters of all parts of the work of the church. Those who give should be educated in churchmanship. Most members of the church know its general work fairly well, and they know the organizations in which they are active. The financial canvass is an opportunity to help them know what parts of the church they may have missed. The alert canvasser will try to enlist support for the program of the church as well as dollars for its budget. Who can tell which is the more important result of a canvass—the dollars that are pledged or growth in churchmanship?

Give everyone, including children and youth, a share in making and meeting the budget

It is a mistake to think that only church officials should help to make the budget and that only adult members should be asked to contribute to it. Some significant thinking is going on about the place of children and youth in the financial practice of the church.

One of the most promising developments in this field is the Youth Budget Plan of the Presbyterian Church in the U.S.A. The Youth Budget represents the contributions of all children and young people to the work of the church. It may be administered by the Westminster Fellowship Council, augmented by teachers representing the kindergarten, primary, and junior departments. Or a Youth Budget Committee may be named, composed of young people representing the junior high, senior high, and older youth age groups, teachers representing the kindergarten, primary and junior departments (with perhaps one or two juniors also) and an adult adviser appointed by the Session through its committee on Christian education. The pastor serves ex officio, and often the church treasurer does also.

This council or committee studies the budget of the church, studies the previous record of youth giving, and determines what portion of the total budget shall be placed before the children and young people as their giving opportunity. The committee then plans for a canvass to secure individual pledges and for the necessary follow-up activities and reports.

All the contributions of children and young people are credited to this budget, regardless of the church group through which the offerings are made. The effect of the Youth Budget Plan has been not only to increase the amount of contributions but to deepen the sense of responsibility which children and young people feel toward the church and its varied ministry.

Move toward the goal of a unified treasury

In the completely unified treasury there is one budget for the whole church, and all contributions to that budget go into a central treasury. Expenses of all church programs and organizations are met through this treasury. This is done either through written orders drawn on the treasury by the officers of each organization or by turning over to each organization the amount specified in the church budget for the work of that organization. All benevolent contributions are made through the central treasurer. The treasurer, therefore, has a record of all benevolent giving, including the contributions of individuals and organizations.

Some advocate doing away altogether with the treasurers of individual organizations. There is justification for this degree of unification, but there is some doubt about it, too. It is a sizable job to keep all the records, pay all the bills, and balance all the accounts in an active church, especially if done by a volunteer treasurer. The job becomes more manageable if some responsibility is held by the organizations. We need to remember, too, that interest and responsibility have a way of going together. It is possible that interest in the work of the church will be reduced if all financial responsibility is taken away from church organizations. Perhaps the solution is for the central treasurer to turn over to each organization monthly the amount due on its budget and let the organization assume responsibility for finances from that point. If the organization plans special activities or benevolent projects, its members must find the way to meet the cost. Regular benevolent contributions, however, should be made through the church treasurer for the sake of proper records.

Base the stewardship program on personal giving rather than on money-raising projects

If the raising of money were the sole aim of stewardship in the church, it would make little difference how the money were raised. The aim of the church, however, is the Christian nurture of persons.

Money is important, for the program of the church cannot be carried on without it. But the way money is raised is more important in the long run. If the budget of the church is raised through serving dinners, selling products, or operating games of chance people will think more about prices, profits, and customers than about persons and their Christian growth.

Adequate Finances for Christian Nurture

Someone must see to it that enough money is provided to support a sound educational program. This responsibility usually rests with the board or committee of Christian education. The board reviews the program which is planned for the coming year. It prepares a budget request in line with that program and submits it to the official body of the church. This budget must include the items which are essential to a complete program of Christian nurture.

Items such as these should be included:

- church school materials, for pupils and teachers
- library additions, including periodicals and resource materials for leaders
- vacation church school
- weekday church school
- leadership education, including subsidy for attendance at camps, conferences, summer leadership schools and workshops
- special programs, such as Promotion Day, Christian Education Week, Children's Day, etc.
- program expenses of fellowship groups of the church
- publicity for educational programs and organizations
- fellowship activities
- postage and stationery
- equipment and supplies
- contributions to local and regional interdenominational agencies
- contributions to denominational enterprises
- contributions to benevolent and social work
- miscellaneous item to cover unexpected expenses

Where there is a director of Christian education, the budget should include funds for attendance at several professional training enterprises each year.

The amounts requested must be large enough to support the educational program adequately. Fluctuating costs make it impossible always to take the budget of the previous year as a guide. The board should be alert to changes in cost of materials. It should be alert to new items that should be included because of new program plans. It is important that the budget request be presented to the official body by someone who is in sympathy with it, and who understands it well enough to secure favorable consideration of it.

CHAPTER X

The Local Church and Its Neighbors

"Let each of you look not only to his own interests, but also to the interests of others. Have this mind among yourselves, which you have in Christ Jesus. . . ."

(Philippians 2:4-5)

* * * * *

It is no accident that one of the two commandments which Jesus selected from among many in the Old Testament was: "You shall love your neighbor as yourself." Except for periods when he went into retreat for meditation and prayer, Jesus was seldom alone. He chose twelve to be with him constantly and to learn from him. He had a larger number of followers, mostly unnamed, who were with him often. Frequently he sought out the company of people who were not his followers at all. Many of his healings and many of his important teachings came when he was with people who were not disciples. The Church of Christ today may well follow the leading of its Master. To fulfill its ministry a church must cultivate warm relationships with its neighbor churches and with agencies that serve the welfare of the community.

The Local Church and Other Churches

In the community

Nearly every church is within easy distance of one or more other Protestant churches. The relationship that exists among them is important. It may range all the way from close co-operation to sharp competition. Through co-operation the churches will find new strength as they help each other, and the community will discover that religion is a power for good. The effect of competition on the internal life of the churches is hard to discover. The aggressive church or the strong church may be further strengthened through competition which causes its members to be on the alert. The small church is likely to suffer from competition. The effect on the community is easier to discover and it is usually bad. Competing churches find it hard to work together, even when they have common concerns. They are sure to impress the community with their division more than with the underlying unity of the Church.

The local council of churches offers the most effective means for neighboring churches to work together. A major purpose of every such council is "to carry on such work of the churches as they desire to be done in co-operation." Every Protestant church should join the local council of churches if there is one. If no council has been established, let the church help to start one.

Every member church should support the local council by contributing to its budget and by promoting its program enterprises. When the council sponsors a program designed to help local churches and their workers, each church should promote that program just as vigorously as if it alone were the sponsor. This assumes, of course, that the program is a good one and that it promises to bring benefits to those who attend. If this should not be the case, the church is under obligation to express its point of view in planning sessions of the council, to the end that future programs may be improved. Among the most helpful educational enterprises that councils have sponsored are leadership schools, vacation church schools, vacation church school institutes, weekday church schools, youth councils, projects in educational evangelism, and specialized workshops and conferences.

Co-operation, however, is not limited to churches working through a council. A few nearby churches in a large city may carry on their own neighborhood projects. So may two or three rural churches in a sparsely settled area. They may work together in the same types of co-operative enterprise as were listed in the preceding paragraph. They may pool their funds to purchase films, filmstrips, audio-visual equipment, and other aids. They will have these resources available for use whenever needed, without the uncertainties that are involved in rental or borrowing. There is no limit to the number of ways in which truly co-operative churches can pool resources. For example, two or three churches may pool their funds and employ a full-time, professionally trained director of Christian education.

In the denomination

Strong ties bind churches of a given denomination to each other. They have the same religious background, and often the same national or racial origin. They have the same organizational pattern and usually the same church school curriculum. Their loyalty is to the same missionary enterprises, and the same educational and benevolent institutions. These ties show plainly why it is usually easy for a church to work closely with others of the same denomination in its region. This regional co-operation has been especially successful in such educational programs as leadership schools, church school workers' conferences related to the denominational curriculum, youth conferences, and workshops related to denominational organizations. Churches of a given denomination frequently call directors of Christian education to serve all the churches in a given area.

The church should think, too, of its relationship to the national denominational program. It should study the recommendations, program suggestions, and curriculum material which denominational agencies prepare. Only through such study can the church know what is available and use this material to best advantage in its program. These materials are geared to the denominational program wherever possible. Therefore, they are more readily useful in churches of that denomination than materials produced elsewhere.

The local church *receives* help through its denomination. It may also *give* help. Editors are constantly looking for stories of successful church projects or activities. The church that has completed a good piece of work should be willing to share its experience. To do this is not vanity or boasting. Publication of the story may help in two ways. It may give an idea to the readers. It may also give assurance to the writers when they discover that their work may benefit others.

The Local Church in the Community

The church and character-building agencies

The average community has a number of character-building agencies. Most of them are not officially sponsored by the churches, but they ought certainly to be allies of the churches. We have in mind such agencies as Boy Scouts, Girl Scouts, Camp Fire Girls, Y.M.C.A., Y.W.C.A., 4-H Clubs, social centers, and welfare agencies of various kinds. How is the church related to them?

It works side by side with them. If there is a community council through which these agencies may consider community affairs, the churches should be represented on the council. Church and agency representatives may then work together for community betterment. If there is no council, let the leaders of churches and of character-building agencies work together in informal co-operation at the points of common interest. Like-minded persons do not have to wait for formal organization in order to support each other.

The local church may sponsor certain character-building agencies. This frequently happens with Boy Scout and Girl Scout troops, and may happen in the case of many other agencies. These church-sponsored agencies work under the general direction of the board of Christian education. If several churches unite in sponsorship, the board should appoint representatives to the administering committee and should receive regular reports from these representatives.

In most communities there are welfare agencies which the church neither sponsors nor controls, nor does it contribute directly to their support. These are the welfare, recreational, and social service agencies which the people of the community support through such means as the Community Chest. The church should help its people know about the work of these agencies and about the benefit they bring to the community. If they do creditable work the church should support them by encouraging church people to join them by publicizing their programs, by endorsing their fund-raising campaigns, and by giving public recognition to church members who give leadership in them.

The church and public schools

Protestant churches and the American public school have grown up together. During the colonial period, and for some years afterward, the teaching of religion was considered a normal function of the school. As more and more people sought the advantages of education, it became clear that public schools would need to serve the entire population. As more and more churches developed, and as differences among them sharpened, it became clear that the schools could not teach religion to satisfy all of them. Therefore the church and the school, as institutions, have gradually been separated.

The church does not attempt to control the policy and program of the school. The school does not attempt to teach specific forms of religion. This policy of separating the institutions of religion and of education, however, does not mean a complete divorce of religion and education. As a matter of fact, neither can be complete without the other. When the schoolman speaks of spiritual values and the churchman speaks of Christianity they are approaching common ground. How can they work together so each is true to his own responsibility, and that together they may serve people and community?

School leaders and church leaders can and should work together as individuals. Neither in his official capacity should try to control the other. They have so many common concerns, however, that it is to everybody's advantage for them to co-operate. They will inevitably work together on some of the same community enterprises. They should become friends. Let them compare ideas about their community and what it needs. Let them work out a strategy by which community conditions may be improved. Let each use his influence to bring about the improvements both want.

Church leaders should respect the law as it bears on relations between church and school. They may feel that laws, and interpretation of laws, leave too little place for religion in the life of the school. This may be so, but it is no reason to flout the law. There are communities in which one religious body includes an overwhelming majority of the people. That religious body is tempted to use its numbers to gain a special place for its beliefs, its practices, its people in the public school. To do so is wrong if it violates the rights of the minority.

Church leaders should help to develop a favorable attitude toward public education. The schools depend on tax funds for most of their continuing budget and for the expansion that is necessary to provide for the increasing numbers of children. To get this support they must have the confidence of the community. In spite of occasional criticism, the great majority of public school teachers and administrators are dedicated to their work, are doing it well, and deserve full support. The church should help them by calling attention to their accomplishments and their needs.

This does not mean that church leaders should ignore criticism of the schools. Let church leaders weigh the criticisms they hear. Those that appear to be valid should be discussed with school administrators before they are aired throughout the community. If the schools are at fault, steps will probably be taken to correct the fault. Invalid criticisms should be stopped as soon as possible.

Churches and schools should work together on their calendars of events so as to avoid serious conflict. It is unfortunate when a child must choose between an important event in the church calendar and an important event in the school calendar. Such agreements as these may emerge from joint planning:

> Keep Sunday free of school activities.
>
> Keep the daytime hours through the week free of church activities for school-age people.
>
> Concentrate church activities for school-age people on one evening, which evening will be free of school events.
>
> Approve a schedule for released-time classes in religion when the churches are prepared to sponsor them.

Be sure that weekday activities of the churches are at least as effective as the public school program for the same age. This applies especially to the weekday church school. Churches are justified in setting up released-time classes only when they can provide a good program and good teaching. This point also applies to any arrangement to clear a given evening for church activities. The churches are under obligation to make good use of that evening. Otherwise they ought to allow the school to use it.

The church and the community in general

The community teaches, and what it teaches has a bearing on the work of the church. In a thousand ways the influence of the community makes itself felt—through radio and television programs that come into the living room; newspapers, magazines and comic books that beg to be read; recreation activities that are available for our spare time; different racial and social groups of the community, together with the way they treat each other. In the welter of community forces the church and its members try to make a consistent Christian witness, supporting what is good and changing what is not good. How may they work to the end that the community may teach for good?

The church should help its members to be informed about community conditions and about the bearing of Christian principles on them. The fellowship groups of the church (youth fellowship, men's organization, women's organization) are well suited to this function. Let them get the facts and then decide for themselves what the Christian strategy is in the light of the facts.

The church should encourage its members to work understandingly for community betterment. It is easy to stand in judgment on the community and point out its faults. Even the best community falls short when measured by Christian standards, and there are times when judgment is what is needed. However, Christians must be willing to come down from the judge's bench and sit in the prisoner's box. They are part of the community. They bear a share of its guilt. They are responsible for its improvement. Let them see the community from the viewpoint of the theater owner, the proprietor of the tavern, the manager of the newsstand. They need not agree with these people, but they must understand before they can help. This willingness to work shoulder-to-shoulder in the community must be part of the strategy that results from the planning that is done in the fellowship groups of the church. All too often the church is so engrossed in perpetuating its own organization that it neglects to co-operate fully with the existing social welfare agencies which seek to serve individuals and improve the community.

The church should use the mass media channels of the community for its message. Television can take religion into the homes of the community just as effectively as it can take drama, sports events, news, and commercials. The same is true of radio, the newspapers, and other community channels. The church that works understandingly with the men who manage these channels of communication will have little trouble in getting opportunity to use them. It is important to remember the caution that when mass media are used for religious purposes, it should be to serve the church as a whole, not to get advantage for one congregation. Furthermore, the church's use of these media must be technically good.

The church should be its own best sermon. We shall not defend this point. Nor shall we elaborate or illustrate it. It is sufficient to say that the church, every time it touches the rest of the community, should be a demonstration of the Christian ethic.

CHAPTER XI

Interpreting the Educational Program

Program planning, organization, administration, and inspired leadership are all basic to Christian nurture. Without them it will not happen, but something else is needed also. People must *know about* the program if they are to participate in it. Therefore the church needs publicity. What people know about the church must make them think well of it. Therefore the church needs its own kind of public relations program. It needs a plan for bringing to people the kind of information that will enable them to understand its program and that will lead them to participate in it and to support it. This kind of plan calls for publicity, but it calls for a good deal more than we usually mean by publicity.

Principles of Public Relations as Applied to Christian Nurture

Remember that the church is its own truest interpreter

What the church *is* speaks more loudly than what it *says*, especially to the newcomer. The church visitor gets a whole battery of first impressions—the building, the people, the way the meeting is conducted, the hymnal, the lesson materials. He likes the church or he does not like it; he wants to be part of the church or he does not; he sees the Christian faith as important to the people of the church or as unimportant—often according to these first impressions. No later announcements or invitations leave as clear an impression as that first visit to a church. The church continues to interpret itself, speaking about its nature to young and old alike, week in and week out.

Compare the silent messages of these two churches as their educational programs speak to people:

Church A—Sturdily built of stone, well maintained; not much space around the building, but well landscaped. At the door a greeter has a ready smile for member and visitor, and he knows how to direct the visitor to the right department. Church school hymnals and lesson materials are suited to the age-group in each department, and are the best available through the denomination. The session is well planned in each department, and most of the classes are well taught. Following the church school is an hour of worship in a well filled sanctuary that speaks its own message through beauty and symbolism.

Church B—Sturdily built of stone, but needs paint; grounds are spacious and well landscaped. The visitor finds his own way to the proper department, in a building that seems strangely out of date in a thriving community. Older children, youth, and adults meet together for an opening session consisting largely of hymns selected at random. The church school hymnal contains many hymns that are bad according to either theological or educational standards. In class after class the teacher does most of the talking while pupils merely sit. In the worship service, the visitor hears a stimulating sermon, but makes a mental note about empty pews and the need of redecoration.

These two churches, as every church, are their own truest interpreters.

In planning any program activity, include plans to publicize and interpret it

If publicity and interpretation are left for later planning, they may come too late. This is a cardinal sin of church school administrators and its effects are seen in low attendance. (See principle on scheduling.)

A more subtle sin is that the planning is disjointed, and the resulting program may be disjointed, too. He who interprets a program necessarily thinks of the people to whom he will interpret it. He must know their interests, their wants, and their needs. If he has a share in planning the program he may call attention to needs and interests that are being overlooked. When the plans are changed to take those needs and interests into account the program will be better and it will be easier to promote.

Be sincere

Is this principle so obvious that it need not be mentioned at all? Perhaps it is, but before reaching this conclusion, the reader should be sure of his answers to two other questions. The first is: *Why do you want to reach people with promotional material?* If the motive is genuine concern for people who need what the church has to offer, that is all well and good. But beware if the motive is statistical! It is all too easy to center attention on growing membership and increasing attendance and to forget that our main concern must be the spiritual growth of people.

The second question is this: *Does your appeal fit the program it seeks to promote?* The only kind of publicity that the church can afford to use is honest publicity. The program which people find in the church should be the kind that the promotion had caused them to expect. If this is so, people have confidence in the church and they support it. If this is not so, the church suffers in the long run, even though it may have increased attendance for a while. There is no excuse for a promotional appeal which cheapens the Christian Church.

Emphasize the positive

Be sure that people know what is good about the program you are interpreting, and what good it will do. Most people are busy, or think they are. They will go to meetings that promise to help them, to help people they care about, or to help the church or community. They will support programs they believe to be good. Therefore be sure to call attention to the positive values of the program you are interpreting.

This emphasis on the positive does not justify ignoring the faults of a program or seeking to gloss them over. Rather, face those faults and correct them. When this has been done you can do vigorous promotion in all sincerity. In the meantime, however, remember that sincerity requires telling the good just as much as it requires recognizing the faults of a program.

Determine the "publics" to be reached

Good publicity calls for more than general announcements which are designed to reach everybody. There are many different "publics" to be reached, and each of them needs to be approached differently.

For example, let us assume that you are responsible for interpreting the camping program of your church. What are your "publics?" You need to get the attention of the *age-groups* for whom camping opportunities are provided (junior, junior high, senior high, post high, young adults, families, and others). They must want to go to camp. Then there are the *parents*. They pay at least part of the bill. They decide whether to urge their children to go, to allow them to go, or to forbid them to go. There are the *teachers* and *counselors* of church groups whose support, tolerance, or opposition will make a difference. There is the *board of Christian education* which sets the church's policy about camping, the *official board* which approves budget, the *pastor* whose influence counts more than that of any other one person. An effective promotional program should aim to reach all of these, and it must reach a majority of them if it is to succeed.

Select the media best suited to reach each "public"

There are many media which may be used to bring information to people. Seldom, if ever, will all of them be used to promote any one event. Each of them has merit, however, and should be used when it will help to interpret the program of the church. The following classification of media under four headings may be helpful:

The spoken word—sermons, addresses, conversation, telephone calls, interview, announcements in meetings, radio.

The printed word—church bulletin, leaflets, brochures, booklets, newspaper announcements and articles, magazines, yearbooks.

Direct mail—letters, postcards, enclosures.

Audio-visual materials—posters, exhibits, films, television, photographs, diagrams, charts, cartoons, billboards, recordings.

There are at least four criteria which will guide the interpreter in selecting the media to use in a particular case.

Suitability. Does the medium fit the program to be interpreted?

Interest. Will it get the attention of the person or group to be reached?

Available skill. Is there a person who can and will use this medium effectively?

Budget. Can you afford it?

Prepare a schedule

Timing is important. It does little good to give people announcements after their schedules have been filled or to give them information after they have already made up their minds. Nor is it good to give announcements and information too soon, for they will be forgotten. Try to give people the kind of information they need at the time they can use it. A good way to be sure that this is done is to prepare a schedule showing the definite times when certain interpretative material will be used.

The following schedule has been suggested for use in leadership schools and will indicate the kind of schedule that may be developed for any program.

Six Months in Advance
- Newspaper release on committees and dates for school

Two Months in Advance
- Letter to key leaders on dates and general plans

One Month in Advance
- Oral announcements in church and community meetings
- Letter to key leaders, enclosing printed flier or bulletin
- Church calendar announcement of dates
- News release on dean and other officers (with pictures)

Three Weeks in Advance
- Oral announcements and church calendar announcements with more details
- Personal calls on key leaders, seeking their support
- News release announcing whom school is for and where to be held

Two Weeks in Advance
- Oral announcements and church calendar announcements with additional details
- Telephone calls to prospective students, if possible
- Radio spot announcements
- News release announcing faculty (with picture of one)

One Week in Advance
- Continue announcements
- News release on courses being offered

One to Two Days in Advance
- News release on special feature or speaker at first session
- Radio interview, television interview

Day Following First Session
- Telephone calls to those missing first session (or letter or card)
- Church calendar announcement on those registered from church
- News release reporting enrollment, speech, or opening feature

One or Two Days in Advance of Remaining Sessions
- Oral announcements
- Telephone calls
- Radio or television spot announcements
- News release on special feature or speaker

Day Following Remaining Sessions
- News release reporting speech or other feature

Follow-up at the End of the School

- Oral reports to sponsoring organization and in church and community meetings
- Letters to key persons reporting results and thanking them for participation
- Church calendar announcement on those completing courses
- News release on day following school[1]

Prepare a folder or booklet about the educational program

It is just as important for a church to prepare a program folder or booklet as it is for a college to print a catalog. The college prints a catalog to tell prospective students and their parents what it offers, because it knows that many people choose a college on the basis of such information. Increasingly people are choosing churches, also, on the basis of the program they offer. How can people know what a church offers unless the church tells them about it? Information about church program is especially important for parents and for newcomers.

The church program booklet should include such information as: location; pictures of building and facilities; denominational relationships; history; organized groups, with purpose, program, or curriculum for the year, officers and leaders, times of meeting; minister and other staff members; official body of the church, standing committees, boards or commissions; services which the church offers to its members and to the community.

The booklet may be large or small, costly or inexpensive, elaborate or simple, printed or mimeographed. Be sure that it tells the story of the church in a way that will be helpful to member and nonmember alike. Let it be in harmony with the church whose program it seeks to interpret.

Review church program and materials, especially from the viewpoint of a newcomer

It may be assumed that a regular member of a church is familiar with the way things are done in it. He knows where the church is, when church school begins, which door to enter, where to go, what comes next in the service, where to find a particular response in the hymnal. But what about the visitor? Are we doing all we can to help him find his way, both in the building and in the program? Will he

---

[1] See *Publicity Strategy*, p. 12-13—Available from the Division of Christian Education of the National Council of Churches.

feel at home? This concern is especially important in a period when many people are moving about. Put yourself in the place of a visitor. Better still, ask a visitor at what points the church can help him to feel at home in it. Then make the changes that are needed in order that everybody may feel at home in your church.

Help each church worker to fulfill his responsibility for public relations

Every person who holds a position in the church has some responsibility for interpreting the church to people. The usher not only receives the offering. He greets people, makes them feel welcome, helps them find a place in the sanctuary where they will feel comfortable. The teacher of a class not only plans lessons and guides the class in learning. He welcomes the visitor. He helps the new member to feel at home and to find a place in the life and work of the class. He interprets many church activities to the class and encourages participation and support. The church school secretary enrolls new members, securing accurate information about them, and placing that information on the proper records of the church. In securing this information he has a chance to tell about the work of the church and, specifically, to show how the information he is requesting will be used.

Thus the public relations responsibility of every officer, teacher, or leader of a church can be identified. It is the responsibility of the administrator to be sure each person understands that responsibility and is helped to fulfill it. This means that the task of interpreting church program must be included in the job description which is discussed with any worker when he is enlisted for special work in the church. It means that training is given as needed, either to individuals or to groups of workers.

Make a united approach wherever possible

Churches near each other often work together in some program or activity. Again, churches may work alone but do the same things at the same times. In all such cases they should co-ordinate their plans for publicity and interpretation. Each can strengthen the other and thus make a stronger impact. If the church page shows that each church is emphasizing the Christian family during Family Week, the reader of the newspaper is bound to be impressed. Also, some media are open to a group of co-operating churches that are not open to churches working separately. For example, a downtown store in a city or large town will seldom permit an individual church to set up a window display. However, the city youth council can almost certainly secure such permission to call attention to Youth Week, if it develops good exhibit materials.

A united approach in publicity speaks to church people and to non-church people alike about the underlying unity of the church. If the public relations efforts of the churches are directed solely toward strengthening each separate church, they may be divisive and weaken the Christian witness. A united approach speaks of unity and declares that the church is concerned about people and their Christian nurture.

Some Implications of These Principles

The principles which we have stated should apply to any effort to publicize or promote the educational program. If this effort is to be really adequate, considerable planning and work are involved. Specific helps for this task may be found in any good manual on publicity or public relations. We shall not attempt to duplicate such material here. Rather, we shall call attention to several "publics" which have a powerful influence on Christian nurture in the church, and to some implications which are involved in interpreting the educational program to them.

The official body of the church

This is the group with final responsibility for policy, program, and budget. The educational administrator should be sure that regular reports are made to it. He should report progress that has been made, plans for the future, needs of people and of program, and questions on which the advice of the official body is desired. Let the reports be varied and graphic. It is well to provide each member with copies of programs and of materials that will help them understand the work being done.

It is important that at least one or two members of this body know the educational program well enough to support it in discussion. Such inside support is vital when there are issues that may involve the future of some part of the educational program. In such cases it is well to do some interpreting before the meeting begins. This may be done by giving reports to members of the body before a meeting so that they may study them at leisure and come to the meeting ready for intelligent discussion. It is often well to discuss important issues ahead of time with key members or with members who are known to have some objection. When questions or objections can be met ahead of time there is less likelihood that they will take up unnecessary time in the meeting or lead to negative action.

Parents

Their sympathetic understanding is important to all church work with children and youth. They decide whether a younger child shall or shall not join in a given program. They determine to a considerable extent the share which the home takes in any form of church-home co-operation.

Three specific approaches to parents are needed in the "average" or larger church. In each of them, remember that the purpose is not merely to "sell" the parents on a particular program, but to secure their informed and interested help in the Christian nurture of their children.

Tell them about future plans and program. This is probably best done through the program booklet which describes the plans of the whole church for the Christian nurture of its people. In most cases this booklet should be mailed to all parents at about the same time.

Arrange for joint planning meetings of group leaders and parents. These meetings aim to report to parents about what has been done and also to get their suggestions and help for the future. Meetings with parents of pre-school children may be held as often as once a month. For this age group teachers and parents should do considerable planning together. Meetings with parents of older children should be held at least quarterly. In youth groups there is more emphasis on reporting and less emphasis on detailed planning, for young people should be largely responsible for working out these plans with their adult teachers and counselors.

Visit in the homes. Each teacher or counselor should visit in each home at least once. Everybody feels more at ease after such a visit. Parents appreciate the interest the church worker takes in their children. The worker is helped by knowing parents and by seeing the homes that are shaping the lives of members of his group. Specific questions and concerns are more likely to come out in personal conversation than in group meeting.

General membership of the church

We have said that the whole church is responsible for Christian nurture. Therefore every member should know what is being done to provide nurture and should help to support it. But every church includes a goodly number of people who are not actively involved in the church's program of Christian nurture. Nor are members of their immediate families actively involved. If these people are to be informed it is important that the church use such general means as church bulletin announcements, the church program booklet, posters about specific events, occasional sermons, and reports in congregational meetings.

An occasional opportunity should be given for the whole congregation to be related to Christian nurture activities. Installation of volunteer workers should take place in a regular public worship service of the church. Recognition of those who have completed leadership courses may be done publicly. Before young people go away to camps or conferences a special service of dedication will be meaningful both to them and to the total congregation. These are only a few suggestions as to what may be done to interpret Christian nurture to the general membership of the church.

The community

The community includes many people who have not joined the church, yet are interested in it and its work. In addition to making a direct approach to those who are on its responsibility list, the church should keep the community informed about its work.

Use newspaper publicity to give well written accounts of significant things that have happened, as well as to make church announcements.

Give radio and television spot announcements of coming events, especially those in which the churches work together. But don't stop with announcements! Provide occasional dramatic programs, interviews with outstanding people, or films and recordings to bring Christian nurture before the whole community.

Posters, car cards, and bulletin board announcements speak to people who never hear a sermon.

Absentee members

Most churches have a fair proportion of members who live too far away for regular participation in church groups. If they have established fixed residence elsewhere, they should be encouraged to join a church in that community. If their absence is temporary, the church should make special effort to keep in touch with them. These temporary absentees include men and women in the armed services, students, people with short-term jobs away from home, and the like.

Appoint individuals or committees to keep in touch with them. Select a person who is interested in students to keep in touch with them, and to provide special opportunities for them when they are home on vacation.

Arrange for two kinds of mail to go to the absentee member. One is general mail, including the church bulletin or newsletter and any special program material that may be developed. The other is personal mail, and it should come from personal friends in the church, especially from members of groups in which the absentee was particularly interested and involved. A loving concern for persons will bridge miles and oceans with Christian fellowship.

CHAPTER XII

Evaluation and Christian Nurture

"How well are we doing?" is a question that everyone who is trying to encourage growth must ask. He must know whether any growth at all is taking place. If there is growth he must know how much. If there is growth at one time rather than at another, it is important for him to know that, for he must do the things that bring growth both rapidly and steadily.

Evaluation is simply the process of getting answers to the question, "How well are we doing?" The process may be difficult. For example, only a skilled physician can tell how well a patient is doing in overcoming an obscure infection. On the other hand, the process may be easy. For example, it is easy to measure growth by marking the height of a child on the door jamb each birthday. Each process whether difficult or easy is an illustration of evaluation. There are many other illustrations—the businessman taking inventory at the close of a year, the school preparing reports and sending them to parents, the nurse taking the temperature and pulse rate of a patient, the television producer checking the popularity of a program. Evaluation is a natural and necessary part of many human enterprises. It is certainly both natural and necessary in Christian nurture.

In Christian nurture we set broad objectives toward which the whole program of the church should help people to grow. We also set specific objectives which are the concern of particular organizations of the church. We set still more specific objectives to be accomplished through a given unit of work or during a single group session. Those who plan programs and lead groups need constantly to know how well people are doing in accomplishing these objectives. The administrator of educational program must, therefore, encourage his fellow-workers in the church to evaluate constantly the results of their work.

The need for constant evaluation also confronts the administrator in the process of program planning. How shall he plan for the future unless he knows the outcomes of past and present program? The administrator finds himself in a program spiral that runs like this: establish goals, plan program to reach the goals, conduct the program, evaluate the results, establish new goals, plan new program, and so on around the spiral. Evaluation, then, is not a process that can be completed once and for all. It becomes a natural part of the work of the administrator in planning and conducting church program, just as it is a natural part of the work of the teacher or group leader.

There are three approaches to evaluation which should be made in every church. We shall examine them under the headings: evaluation of church program, tests and their use in church groups, and evaluation of individual status and growth.

Evaluation of Church Program

It is well to ask ourselves occasionally how well we are doing in the program of the church as a whole or in such an agency as the Sunday church school. How shall we go about it?

General indications

There are some general indications that come to us without any difficulty at all. One of them is *membership*. Is it increasing, static, or decreasing? The answer to this question tells us something about how well we are doing.

Attendance is another. Is it increasing, static, or decreasing? Is it regular or irregular? Is the situation with respect to membership and attendance the same throughout the church or is it better in some organizations and age groups than in others?

Participation is another general indication. Do people accept office or responsibility willingly or is it necessary to use pressure? Does the work of the church rest largely on a few people or is it widely shared? Is the record of participation the same throughout the church, or is there more participation in some groups and less in others?

A fourth general indication is *finance*. Does the church meet its local obligations easily? How willingly and freely does the church contribute to benevolent causes? Do church contributions come largely from the wealthier members, or is there a broad base of financial support?

These general indications may provide significant evaluations with regard to the church's success in Christian nurture. It is necessary, however, to probe beneath the surface. If attendance and membership are static or decreasing, find out why. Then decide how the weaknesses may be corrected. Even if membership and attendance are increasing, try to find whether the increase is sufficient. In a period of population increase, the active church should be growing more rapidly than the population as a whole.

A slowly growing church in a mushrooming community is not doing as well as a church that holds its own in a declining community. Probe beneath the surface of these general indications, and then be guided by these deeper findings.

Study the records

The records and reports of the church help us know how well we are doing, if we study them. No one can predict what the study of records and reports in a particular church may show. There are, however, some things that it is well to look for.

Compare attendance and membership. If there have been marked increases or decreases, find out why. If one organization or group differs markedly from another, find out why. If attendance in particular groups is irregular, find out why.

Study the length of service of leaders in different church groups. There may be a connection between vitality of the group and the length of time the present leadership has served. There are values in continuity of service and values in change. There are dangers in each. What does the record show?

Study programs of the church and of its groups and discover their effect on membership, attendance, offerings, and the like.

These are just a few of the ways in which a study of records and reports may help in evaluation.

Standards and rating scales

A standard is a measuring device intended to serve as an aid in evaluating and improving program. It sets up a pattern which is generally considered to be good in order that a given church or group may compare itself with that pattern. The most commonly accepted standard at present is *The International Standard for the Sunday Church School.* It considers the work of the church school under four headings: Curriculum, Leadership, Organization and Administration, and Housing and Equipment. Each of these four broad areas is divided into its more important divisions—nineteen in all. Each division is introduced by a brief statement which shows clearly what is meant by it. Then follows, for each division, a list of questions. The answer to each question shows how well the church under consideration is measuring up to good practice in Christian nurture. A scoring chart is provided, with a maximum score of 500. By use of the chart one can see at a glance the extent to which his own church school measures up to the standard.

In most churches this *Standard* may be used to best advantage in the workers' conference. The actual scoring may be done by the conference as a whole or by a committee appointed for the purpose. The entire group should have opportunity, however, to discuss the results and to consider the steps that should be taken toward improvement.

Three factors should be kept in mind in selecting points at which to undertake improvements. One is the items on which the rating was lowest. These are clearly points where the program is weak. A second is the items that are crucial. The church school will suffer from neglect of these items, even though they may not be the lowest items on the scoring chart. A third factor is that of practicability. Which are the items on which improvement can be made quickly and easily? It is good to do something where results will show soon and will, therefore, encourage people to undertake other improvements.

Some denominations have developed standards which are especially suited to their own churches. Rating scales have been prepared for use with certain types of workers such as the church school teacher or with certain organizations such as the youth fellowship. The administrator should secure copies of these instruments and discuss their use with workers in his church. Information as to what standards are available may be secured either through the denominational board of Christian education or through the National Council of Churches. In any case, what is most important is not the score that is worked out but the improvement that results. Sometimes the new understanding that comes from use of the standard outweighs all the other results.

Get member reaction

The way members feel about a group and its program provides a most important kind of evaluation. The trouble is that people often conceal their true feelings about the groups to which they belong. Or at least they conceal their true feelings from the leaders of those groups. The question of the administrator, then, is how to find out the way people really feel about a group.

One way is to watch them. The role a person plays in a group may range all the way from active participation, through various degrees of indifference, to actual opposition. His feelings may range all the way from enjoyment, through various degrees of neutrality, to keen dislike. The alert leader will discover some of these reactions merely by watching members of a group.

A second way is to let them tell it. This may be done by direct questions as to how they feel about the group and its program. More often it is done indirectly, as members of the group share in decisions about program and activity. If they feel free to suggest what they really want, evaluation and planning will take place at the same time, and this is good. On the other hand, if the leader regards any suggestion as a criticism of him people will hesitate, and the things they say will not represent honest evaluation.

A third way is to let them write it. Increasing use is being made of simple blanks to get member reaction. These blanks are filled out and returned unsigned, in order to encourage maximum frankness. The blank may include a general item such as this: "In my experience, the youth fellowship fulfills its purpose fully_____; largely_____; fairly well_____; a little_____; not at all_____." Then may follow a number of suggestions with provision for each person to check the suggestions he approves. There should always be space for the individual member to add further suggestions of his own. It may be better to list no specific suggestions but to encourage each member to write in his own.

To secure member reaction is not a sign of weakness or uncertainty on the part of the leader. It is a sign that the leader is big enough and secure enough to allow the group to enjoy leadership, to make changes, and take initiative.

Evaluation in Church Groups

Evaluation is not simply a procedure used to check on the general direction and effectiveness of church work. It may be used to good advantage with a given group as a means of involvement and of growth. Such evaluation is especially useful at the beginning or at the end of a unit of work or of experience. When a church school class begins a new curriculum unit it is important for the teacher to find out at least four things: what the members of the class know about the new subject, how they feel about it, what they are already doing about it, and what needs or interests they have which relate to it. At the close of the unit it is good to find out what changes have taken place in knowledge, feeling, and behavior. The teacher who thinks mostly of content may outline his plans without feeling the need for evaluation at all. One of the functions of the administrator, then, is to help teachers sense the need for evaluation. Another function is to help teachers find out the things mentioned above.

The department planning conference provides an excellent opportunity to help teachers feel the need for studying their pupils in relation to a new unit. The leader may raise the question as to what the pupils know, feel, and do about the new subject. The lack of real information will probably be obvious. If so, the group may move naturally to ways of getting this information.

The administrator should know enough about the different ways of evaluation to encourage group leaders to use them. For this purpose we list the ways in most frequent use, with a brief description of each.

Direct questions

They may help both to introduce a new unit and to discover the status of pupils with respect to it. Questions may be answered on the spur of the moment, or they may be answered at greater length in writing. The spoken answer is more useful to the teacher and more popular with pupils! The church school teacher's manual usually suggests appropriate questions. Such questions can scarcely provide a complete evaluation of pupil status regarding the new unit because the teacher cannot ask enough questions to cover the whole unit, and because most of the answers will come from the better-informed pupils. Though direct questions will not provide a complete or scientifically accurate evaluation of the knowledge and attitude of pupils, they will give the teacher a great deal of helpful information.

Interest finders

These are usually prepared in the form of check lists. Possible subjects for group programs or for class discussion are listed, with opportunity for members to check those in which they are particularly interested. If the items are selected properly the compiled results will give a good idea of group interest.

Range-of-opinion statements

The range-of-opinion statement is a device which helps to locate individual or group opinion on complicated quotations. These questions usually involve issues to which a Yes-or-No answer cannot readily be given. Some evidence indicates a "Yes" answer, and some evidence points to "No." The true answer, therefore, lies somewhere between the two. The following series of statements reflecting a range of opinion regarding the church is an example:

The Church is a divine institution, and it commands my highest loyalty and respect.

The Church is a fellowship of people drawn together by their common commitment to Jesus Christ.

The Church is an institution which has lifted the level of personal and social life through the centuries.

The Church is a human institution, and is as good or as bad as its members make it.

I have nothing but contempt for the Church.

Such a series of statements can be used in at least two ways. Members of a group may be asked to check the statements with which they agree. The findings may then be summarized and reported as a measure of group opinion and as a basis for discussion.

The series of statements may also be used to clarify opinion through discussion. Each person reads the series and then selects the statement he prefers. Pros and cons of the different statements are discussed as each indicates the factors that led to his decision. In the process new insights emerge and opinions are clarified. There is no attempt to force the group to agree on any one statement. Opinions are located as a basis for discussion and for deepened understanding.

Objective tests

Various types of paper and pencil tests which are in common use are known as objective tests because they can be scored objectively. They are arranged so the scoring is done according to definite standards, not according to opinion.

Recall tests

The pupil is given statements which require a brief addition in order to make them complete sentences. For example:

The disciple who betrayed Jesus was ______________.

Completion tests

These are much like Recall tests, except that there are more blanks to be filled. For example: __________ led the children of Israel out of ____________ and to the borders of the __________________ land.

Matching tests

The pupil is asked to indicate which items in two separate lists or columns belong together. In the following illustration, he may be asked to place a number in each of the blanks in column A to identify the item that matches a corresponding item in column B.

A	B
__Judas	1. First book in New Testament
__David	2. Disciple who betrayed Jesus
__Moses	3. Led children of Israel out of Egypt
__Paul	4. The Psalmist
__Matthew	5. The writer of Epistles

True-false tests

A series of statements is prepared, about half being false and the other half true. The pupil is asked to mark each statement as either true or false.

Multiple-choice tests

Statements are prepared showing a number of responses that may be made. The pupil selects the one he considers right. One answer is clearly right, and the others as clearly wrong. A variant of the multiple-choice test is that in which opinions are given and the pupil selects the one he regards as best. A multiple-choice test item might be the following:

The first book in the New Testament is Genesis, Matthew, John, Romans.

Shall We Use Prepared Tests or Develop Our Own?

A number of standardized tests are available in the field of religion. They have been used widely enough to have proved their reliability. Norms have been established so that a leader may have a rough idea as to how his group compares with the average for a given age-group. These tests are extremely helpful when they are used by a trained person, and when they relate closely enough to the current program of the church so that the findings will be useful. The number of these tests in current use, however, does not seem to be increasing.

There does seem to be an increase in tests that are directly related to the church school curriculum. The curriculum-related test may be prepared either by a curriculum writer or by someone in the local church. In either case its initial purpose is to help the teacher find where pupils stand regarding a new unit, or to find what progress has been made in an on-going unit. This kind of test has immediate meaning to both pupil and teacher. Immediate use can be made of its findings.

The teacher should exercise care in preparing the test items to be sure that they are clear in meaning. If the test is given at the beginning of a new unit, it should contain some items easy enough for any member of the class to answer, and some items so hard that none can answer them. It should include enough items to reveal weaknesses in understanding that can be dealt with as the unit progresses.

Workers interested in using standardized tests should write for information about them to the denominational board of Christian education or to the Department of Research of the Division of Christian Education of the National Council of Churches. Those interested in testing in relation to curriculum will find their best help in the teacher's manuals. For further information they should write to the denominational board of Christian education.

Evaluation and the Individual

The conscientious leader is bound to ask himself how far he shall go in testing individual status and growth. He recognizes that Christian nurture deals primarily with individuals. The final purpose of work in church groups is to help the individuals in those groups. Evaluation of church work, therefore, boils down to evaluation of the individual.

The teacher of a church school class should do at least three things in order to fulfill his responsibility. He should observe the responses and behavior of each person in the class. When tests are given he should score each individual's work separately and make note of points where individual help is needed. He should keep his own confidential record, as suggested in an earlier chapter. This record should include the teacher's interpretation of observation and tests, for that interpretation will show what the teacher feels should be done to help the person.

Whenever a member of the group shows need of particular help, the teacher should secure the results of other evaluations. He should confer with public school teachers to get the benefit of their evaluation of these individuals. He should confer with the pastor and any others in the church who may have information to share. He should check with leaders of club groups in which the member has been involved.

He goes as far in the use of these findings as his time and training will allow and as the need of the individual suggests. When he approaches the limits of his time and ability, he turns to other persons. He brings their ability as well as his own to bear on the person. He knows that the pastor has a responsibility as pastor and counselor. He knows that social workers have both responsibility and training that some of his pupils may need. He does not stand in their way, but he does his best to bring to bear the interests and abilities of all of them together for the sake of a person who needs to grow toward Christian maturity.

When all is said and done, the leader of any church group knows himself as the ambassador of God who "so loved the world that he gave his only Son, that whoever believes in him should not perish but have eternal life."

References Used by the Author

The author wishes to express appreciation to the writers and publishers of the following resources.

CHAPTER I

Goals for the Christian Education of Children. New York: National Council of Churches.

Junior High Objectives. New York: National Council of Churches.

CHAPTER II

Christian Education Today. New York: National Council of Churches.

CHAPTER III

Education of Christian Parents in America. New York: National Council of Churches.

CHAPTER IV

The Board of Christian Education in the Local Church (Leaflet) New York: National Council of Churches.

Case, William F. *A Democratic Conception of the Administration of the Local Church.* (Doctoral dissertation completed at Columbia University, unpublished at the date of this writing.)

Church School Administration Filmstrips. New York: National Council of Churches.

CHAPTER V

Case, William F. (see title above)

A Guide for Curriculum in Christian Education. New York: National Council of Churches.

Tower, Howard E. *Church Use of Audio-Visuals.* Nashville: Abingdon Press.

Using Audio-Visuals in the Church. New York: National Council of Churches.

Audio-Visual Resource Guide for Use in Religious Education. New York: National Council of Churches.

Organization and Administration of Christian Education in the Local Church. New York: National Council of Churches.

CHAPTER VI

Leadership Education Handbook. New York: National Council of Churches.

And Gladly Serve. New York: National Council of Churches.

Third Series Work of the Standard Leadership Curriculum (Educational Bulletin 503). New York: National Council of Churches.

The Laboratory School Manual. New York: National Council of Churches.

Gwynn, Price H., Jr. *Leadership Education in the Local Church.* Philadelphia: Westminster Press.

Haiman, Franklyn S. *Group Leadership and Democratic Action.* New York: Houghton Mifflin Company.

The Leadership Education Audio-Visual Kit (10 filmstrips) New York: National Council of Churches.

Calendar of Leadership Education Activities (leaflet) New York: National Council of Churches.

Chapter VII

Increasing Attendance. New York: National Council of Churches.

Chapter VIII

Kramer, Emma J. *Equipment and Arrangement for Children's Groups in the Church.* New York: National Council of Churches.

Making the Most of Rooms and Equipment (filmstrip in the Leadership Education Audio-Visual Kit). New York: National Council of Churches.

Chapter IX

Youth Budget Program Guide. New York: Presbyterian Church in the U.S.A.

Chapter X

Vieth, Paul H. *The Church and Christian Education.* St. Louis: Bethany Press. (Chapters VII, VIII.)

Chapter XI

Publicity Strategy. New York: National Council of Churches.

Stuber, Stanley. *Public Relations Manual for Churches.* New York: Doubleday and Co., Inc.

Chapter XII

International Standard for the Sunday Church School. New York: National Council of Churches.

Improving the Total Program of Your Church. New York: National Council of Churches.

Bibliography

ARBAUGH, GEORGE B. *Growth of a Christian.* Philadelphia: The Muhlenberg Press, 1952.

FRANK, LAWRENCE K. *How to Be a Modern Leader.* New York: Association Press, 1954.

GWYNN, PRICE H., JR. *Leadership Education in the Local Church.* Philadelphia: Westminster Press, 1952.

HEIM, RALPH D. *Leading a Sunday Church School.* Philadelphia: The Muhlenberg Press, 1950.

MCKIBBEN, FRANK M. *Guiding Workers in Christian Education.* Nashville: Abingdon Press, 1953.

MCRAE, GLENN. *Teaching Christian Stewardship.* St. Louis: Bethany Press, 1954.

MILLER, RANDOLPH C. *The Clue to Christian Education.* New York: Scribners, 1950.

REYNOLDS, FERRIS E. *An Adventure with People.* Philadelphia: The Christian Education Press, 1954.

SCHISLER, JOHN Q. *Christian Teaching in the Churches.* Nashville: Abingdon Press, 1954.

SMART, JAMES D. *The Teaching Ministry of the Church.* Philadelphia: Westminster Press, 1954.

TOWER, HOWARD E. *Church Use of Audio-Visuals.* Nashville: Abingdon Press, 1950.

WYCKOFF, D. CAMPBELL. *The Task of Christian Education.* Philadelphia: Westminster Press, 1955.

"Leadership Education Calendar." New York: National Council of Churches.

"Local Church Board of Christian Education." New York: National Council of Churches.

"Your Church Library." New York: National Council of Churches.